# A MOMENT OF TRANSITION

## Two Neuroscientific Articles by Sigmund Freud

# A MOMENT OF TRANSITION

## Two Neuroscientific Articles by Sigmund Freud

edited and translated by

*Mark Solms and Michael Saling*

The Institute of Psycho-Analysis

London

1990

Routledge
Taylor & Francis Group

LONDON AND NEW YORK

*to Sidney Press*

First published 1990 by Karnac Books Ltd.

2 Park Square, Milton Park, Abingdon, Oxfordshire OX14 4RN
52 Vanderbilt Avenue, New York, NY 10017

*Routledge is an imprint of the Taylor & Francis Group, an informa business*

First issued in paperback 2019



**British Library Cataloguing in Publication Data**
Freud, Sigmund, *1856–1939*
A moment of transition: two neuroscientific articles.
1. Neuropsychology
I. Title II. Solms, Mark III. Saling, Michael
152

ISBN 978-0-946439-92-8 (pbk)
ISBN 978-0-367-32389-9 (hbk)

*CONTENTS*

PART THREE
## Exposition

# *FOREWORD*

## *Mortimer Ostow*

World War II, and especially the Holocaust that accompanied it, drove the centre of ferment of psychoanalysis from Central Europe, where it had originated, to England and the United States—the English-speaking world. As a result it became necessary to provide accurate English translations of the foundation works of psychoanalysis, Freud's essays and books, as well as the contributions of his disciples. These translations have been undertaken by a series of dedicated and gifted individuals, for whose efforts we are grateful. Of course the papers first translated were those that bore directly upon clinical practice and its supporting theory. Only latterly have the works of primarily historical interest been presented to the English-speaking public. Nevertheless, as Solms and Saling note, many of Freud's neurological works remain untranslated, so that English readers are deprived of the opportunity to see Freud functioning as a neurologist and then turning his interest to psychopathology, on the way to the evolution of psychoanalysis. Solms has undertaken to provide a series of English translations of Freud's hitherto untranslated neurological papers, the first two of which are presented in this volume.

As the reader will observe, the work of translation has been carried out with an unusual degree of meticulousness, faithfully rendering even complex thoughts into clear, lucid, unambiguous, and easily readable English.

The translator and his associate, Michael Saling, have provided also a thoroughgoing discussion of the origin of these pre-analytical articles, what they reveal to us about the scientific climate in which Freud worked, how his work and ideas related to those of his contemporaries, and how they can be seen as steps on the road to the discipline of psychoanalysis. They also confront various challenges that have been posed to psychoanalysis in recent decades, that are based upon claims that Freud was limited by the archaic and dated views of central nervous system function that prevailed in his time. The authors demonstrate decisively Freud's departure from the conventional wisdom and the development of his original ideas.

We are treated to a view of the thinking of the most distinguished neuropsychiatrist of history as he disappointingly comes to grips with the fact that neurological studies offer no window onto the discipline of psychopathology. On the contrary, Freud observed, psychological considerations must be taken into consideration in anatomical and physiological theorizing. For example, in the 'Aphasie' article, on the basis of clinical observation of aphasic speech disorders, he rejects the localization theories of aphasia, the concept that various 'speech centres' each controls a specific aspect of speech, proposing instead a 'speech field', a broad area in which the operations subserving speech are carried on. Lesions in specific regions impair those operations in somewhat specific ways because they impinge upon fibres passing through these regions, but one is not justified to infer that these regions are discrete speech centres in the sense that they are concerned with the psychological formulation or control of speech. In this respect, Freud anticipated important developments in twentieth-century aphasiology and is considered by the editors of this volume to be one of the founding fathers of modern neuropsychology.

The 'Gehirn' article demonstrates cogently Freud's dynamic mode of thinking, so that even his description of the gross neuroanatomy of the brain takes the form of an exploration rather than a colourless exposition. I refer to Freud as a neuropsychiatrist deliberately, because until recent decades, neurology and psychiatry were practised by the same individual, the assumption being that knowledge of the one would facilitate the practice of the other, and that the knowledge of brain anatomy and physiology would facilitate the practice of both. For similar reasons, obstetrics and gynaecology are frequently practised together to this day. Freud was a neuropsychiatrist. So was Meynert, and so was Charcot. The psychoanalytical reader will recognize the name of Paul Flechsig, whose neuroanatomical investigations Freud quotes admiringly, as the psychiatrist who cared for Daniel Paul Schreber.

In practice, the two disciplines are approached independently. In the second half of the nineteenth century, their interests coincided primarily in the case of dementia paralytica and of focal lesions of the brain, traumatic, vascular, or neoplastic. In our day, psychopharmacological theory has been promising to promote a fruitful exchange between neurophysiology and neurochemistry on the one hand, and psychiatric theory on the other, but at this time, psychopharmacology remains an empirical discipline.

Sigmund Freud, like the other scholarly neuropsychiatrists of his time, seems to have been beguiled by the hope that neuroanatomy could illuminate psychical function. He was disappointed. In the two essays in this book I was able to find only two examples of a claimed relation between these areas. In the one instance, Freud observed that the commissures and decussations of the brain 'link equivalent cortical elements of the two hemispheres with each other and . . . place experiences delivered by the senses of the two bilaterally symmetrical body-halves in the kind of relationship with each other that enables them to appear within the unitary point of view of ego consciousness' (p. 66, this volume). In the second instance, Freud, following Meynert, calls the fibres linking parts of the cerebral cortex to each other, association fibres, 'because they serve the association of ideas' (ibid.).

Despite these exceptions, Freud seems to be giving up the hope of correlating brain structure with mental life. Mental activity, he suggests, is a superordinate function with access to consciousness and which controls the access to consciousness of material changes in brain function. Specific changes in brain function may be associated with specific mental states, but those mental states are not guaranteed access to consciousness. Freud acknowledges, in other words, that mental state can be influenced by brain function, but that it also retains its independence.

> If the same brain element undergoes the same change of state at different times, then the corresponding mental process can be linked with it on one occasion (it can cross the threshold of consciousness), [at] another time not. For the present we are unable to formulate the ruling over the laws governing this [any] closer. We don't know whether or not the ruling only depends, apart from [depending upon] the change in the state of the considered elements, upon the simultaneous state and changes in the state of other brain elements, or moreover, also depends upon still something else. [pp. 62, 63, this volume]

He says clearly that he does not know how to relate brain function to psychical function. We see him here cutting his psychology loose from neuroanatomy and neurophysiology. Nevertheless, in his 1891 essay on aphasia, he comes out clearly for psychophysical parallelism (see Jones, 1953, p. 403).

Evidently the transition from the search for a material basis for psychological and psychopathological phenomena to the determination to formulate a theory of mental events in their own terms was not a smooth one. In the *Cocaine Papers* (Freud, 1884–87), which were written just before these two pre-analytical articles, we find splendid clinical descriptions of the effects of cocaine and suggestions about its clinical utility, but almost no attempt to contrive any kind of psychological description or theory.

In the same encyclopedia in which these two pre-analytical papers were published, Freud also published an article on hysteria (1888b3), in which he makes no attempt to relate its symptoms to brain structure or function, although he writes that:

> Hysteria is based wholly and entirely on physiological modifications of the nervous system and its essence should be expressed in a formula which took account of the conditions of excitability in the different parts of the nervous system. [ibid., p. 41]

In 1886, Freud announced that he was preparing a paper on 'Some points for a comparative study of organic and hysterical motor paralyses' (1893c). Presumably it was written soon after the cocaine papers and almost simultaneously with the two papers in this volume. Here he proposes perhaps the first description of what has come to be called 'structure' in psychoanalytical theory—namely, an enduring complex of psychical function, in this case, the conception of a thing. He uses the term 'functional or dynamic lesion' to refer to 'the abolition of the associative accessibility of the concept of the arm'. This inaccessibility is caused by a trauma which endows the complex with a 'quota of affect' that it cannot dissipate. He emphasizes that the conception can become inaccessible 'without being destroyed and without its material substrate (the nervous tissue of the corresponding region of the cortex) being damaged.' Here we see the beginning of psychoanalytical theorizing, but with some reference back to accompanying neural structure and changes.

Meanwhile, in 1891, Waldeyer gave final form to the neurone theory. The word 'neurone' appears in Freud's 1893 paper, followed by a parenthetical definition, 'cellulo-fibrillary neural unit'. With the concept of the neurone, Freud saw an opportunity to revive his quest to base his psychology on knowledge of the structure of the nervous system. He forsook gross anatomy for a feature of microscopic anatomy. But he realized intermittently that he was not building upon true anatomy and physiology, but only on a fairly gross and simplistic schematic hypothesis.

> Anyone, however, who is engaged scientifically in the construction of hypotheses will only begin to take his theory seriously if they can be fitted into our knowledge from more than one direction and if the arbitrariness of a *constructio ad hoc* can be mitigated in relation to them. [1950a (1895), p. 302]

Freud was evidently trying to overcome his own doubts. It is not surprising therefore to learn that during the year 1895 he alternately worked feverishly on the Project and abandoned it. Speaking of the prospect of working out a psychology, Freud wrote to Fleiss in May 1895,

> It has beckoned to me from afar, since time immemorial, but now that I have met with the neuroses it has come that much nearer. I am vexed by two intentions: to discover what form the theory of psychical functioning will take if a quantitative line of approach, a kind of economics of nervous force, is introduced into it. . . . [ibid., editor's introduction, p. 283]

Focusing on the usefulness of the 'energy' concept, Freud, in the 'Project', ignored almost completely the complex gross structure of the nervous system, the knowledge of which he demonstrates and communicates so skilfully in 'Gehirn'. He differentiates between sensory and motor nerves, between the superficial and deeper layers of the cortex, and among the various sensory reception areas (ibid., p. 315). Otherwise he treats the brain as a homogeneous structure, composed of a collection of small objects, which he calls neurones, all of which have the same properties. He does not allow for variation among them in these properties, nor for spontaneous activity internally generated. By discarding the manuscript, he tried to terminate this attempt to relate psychology to brain function permanently.

The 'energy' factor has run like a red thread from Freud's earliest thoughts about psychology and psychopathology until the last. In 'Gehirn' he speaks of the 'specific energy' of sensory nerves (p. 65, this volume). He refers here to qualities of sensation and uses a concept propagated by Helmholtz, one that invokes the energy concept. He concludes his early paper on hysteria (1888b3) with the comment that

> hysteria is an anomaly of the nervous system which is based on a different distribution of excitations, probably accompanied by a surplus of stimuli in the organ of the mind. Yet symptomatology shows that this surplus is distributed by means of conscious or unconscious ideas. Anything that alters the distribution of the excitations in the nervous system may cure hysterical disorders: such effects are in part of a physical and in part of a directly psychical nature. [ibid., p. 57]

In his final and uncompleted work on psychoanalytical theory, *An Outline of Psycho-analysis* (1940a), Freud wrote:

> The future may teach us to exercise a direct influence by means of particular chemical substances on the amounts of energy and their distribution in the mental apparatus. [p. 182]

I believe that in that statement he was thinking back to his experiences with cocaine, restating his persistent belief in the importance of an energy factor in psychology, and anticipating the mode of action of other psychopharmacological agents. It is of no importance that his earliest thoughts about energy dealt with measurable conduction processes in nerves and his later thoughts with a non-material, hypothetical parameter of psychical function. In both instances he was concerned about motivation and its disturbances. The energy factor was a quantitative concept that governed variation in motivation and that lent itself to theoretical, metapsychological elaboration as well as to the concept of being influenced by chemical agents.

Given the puzzles of nature, each time a new scientific methodology or discipline becomes available, it is immediately turned to the attempt to solve outstanding problems. In this century, attempts have been made to comprehend psychical function and its relation to brain function by the application of theories of electrical conduction, reverberating circuits, feedback mechanisms, computer analogies, humoral influences (neurotransmitters), neurobiology, molecular biology, immunology, ethology, and neuronal group selection. They are all powerful tools, and each contributes something to our understanding of the relation between brain function and psychical function. But the definitive resolution seems as remote as ever.

Meanwhile, psychoanalysis has flourished. Its theories, the fundamentals of which were established by Freud, have been elaborated, altered and simplified, challenged and defended. Yet Freud's psychological vocabulary and concepts, initial intimations of which appeared one hundred years ago in the two articles of this book (satisfaction of needs; aim presentation; word presentation; ideas of external objects; need satisfaction by imaginary action) and basic psychoanalytical theory have been heard around the world and have been applied in most disciplines of the humanities. Practice has changed less than theory and is probably more consistent among different psychoanalytical communities. While in some locations the demand for psychoanalytical treatment has diminished and authentic analysis has been displaced to some extent by inauthentic analysis and by other therapies, psychoanalysis has contributed to a host of psychodynamic therapies, so that its influence has grown greatly. The theories and techniques of analysis have been informed and amplified by infant and child observation, by the application of analysis and its derivatives to more disturbed patients, by the accumulation of clinical data.

The dynamic that Freud saw one hundred years ago was that psychology had to be disengaged from the anatomy and physiology that was then available and permitted to develop on its own, and then in developed form slowly recruited to re-engage a far more subtle and sophisticated anatomy, physiology, pharmacology, and chemistry. As he has taught us in other contexts, needs can often best be satisfied if they are temporarily renounced. Psychoanalysis, Freud said twenty years after these papers were written,

> hopes to discover the common ground on the basis of which the convergence of physical and mental disorder will become intelligible. With this aim in view, psycho-analysis must keep itself free from any hypothesis that is alien to it, whether of an anatomical, chemical or physiological kind, and must operate entirely with purely psychological auxiliary ideas. . . . [Freud, 1916–17, p. 21]

In these papers we see the beginning of that renunciation and disengagement; they give us a glimpse of this crucial moment, the preparation for the application of the psychoanalytical method to the resolution of problems of human psychology. We are impatient to initiate the process of reengagement, but it continues to elude us.

# *PREFACE*

When one considers the enormous and enduring impact of Sigmund Freud's work on twentieth-century science and culture and the continuing fascination with his life and ideas, it is indeed remarkable to discover that a large portion of his writings still remain inaccessible to the English-speaking reader. Between 1877 and 1900, Freud published over one hundred neuroscientific works, but only seven of these have ever appeared in English translation. This is especially remarkable in view of the acknowledged fact that Freud was an important pioneer in many neuroscientific fields, and all the more so in view of the enormous body of recent literature on the influence of his early neurological background upon his later psychoanalytical work. This latter body of literature in particular has failed to take account of more than one or two works from Freud's neurological writings, and one must assume that this selectivity is at least in part due to the fact that so few of the neuroscientific works are yet available in English. In publishing the present book we seek to go some way towards correcting this source of potential error and bias in the scholarly and scientific evaluation of Freud's pre-analytical writings.

We conducted the research for this book during 1985–86, and the manuscript was completed in all essentials by early 1987. Its publication has been delayed by a variety of unavoidable external circumstances. We now owe a belated debt of gratitude to the following people and organizations: Ferdinand Schaub, for his generous help with the early drafts of the translations; Dagmar Erken, for her correction of the later drafts; Karen Kaplan-Solms, for her many helpful comments on the expository aspect; Annesu de Vos and Oliver Turnbull, for their meticulous preparation of the manuscript; Mark Paterson and Jo Richardson of Sigmund Freud Copyrights, for their assistance towards the authorization of the translations and for granting us permission on behalf of the Freud beneficiaries to publish them; and Joachim Niendorf and Ferdinand Enke Verlag, for their very gracious attitude in the matter of ownership of copyright. Thanks are also due to Cesare Sacerdoti of Karnac Books, Peter Fonagy of The Institute of Psycho-Analysis, and Klara Majthényi King, copy-editor, for bringing this project to final fruition.

# A MOMENT OF TRANSITION

Two Neuroscientific Articles
by Sigmund Freud

*PART ONE*

# Introduction

*SECTION ONE*

# Scope and objectives of the study

This book presents authorized English translations of two relatively unknown German articles that are believed to have been written by Sigmund Freud, and it seeks to establish their significance for psychoanalysis and neuroscience. The two articles, entitled 'Aphasie' and 'Gehirn', were originally published in 1888 in the first part of a two-volume medical dictionary edited by Albert Villaret, the *Handwörterbuch der gesamten Medizin* (Villaret, 1888/1891).

There has recently been much intellectual and scientific interest in Freud's pre-psychoanalytical, neuroscientific work. Up to now, however, most of this interest has centred around only two texts. Neuroscientists have concentrated on Freud's (1891b) monograph *On Aphasia*, and psychoanalysts have focused their attention on the 'Project for a scientific psychology' (Freud, 1950a [1895]).[1] The vast bulk of Freud's neuroscientific works still remain untranslated.[2] The Institute of Psycho-Analysis and The Hogarth Press had recently intended to publish them in a three-volume set, entitled *The Pre-Analytical Works of Sigmund Freud*, but were compelled to abandon the project (Charlton, personal communication, 25 March 1985). The translations presented in this book are therefore the first. The intention behind their publication is to broaden the base of primary source material for the scholarly evaluation of Freud's pre-analytical, neuroscientific period.

The book is organized according to the following plan: part one begins with a brief description of 'Aphasie' and 'Gehirn'. These two articles were unsigned, and therefore there has been some doubt as to whether they were, in fact, written by Freud. In view of the obvious importance of this issue for our purposes, this question of authorship is addressed second. Third, the existing body of literature on the articles is reviewed. Fourth, the potential contribution of the two articles to Freud scholarship is discussed. In part two, after a brief discussion on our rendition of some controversial terms, the translations themselves are presented. In the third and final part, the articles are comprehensively and critically evaluated with respect to their significance both for psychoanalysis and for neuroscience.

## NOTES

1. In order to distinguish between the 'Project for a scientific psychology' and the German and English editions of the Freud–Fliess correspondence (which included the 'Project'), these are referred to here as Freud (1950a[1895]), (1950a), and (1954), respectively.
2. Apart from *On Aphasia* (Freud, 1891b) and the 'Project' (Freud, 1950a[1895]), only Freud's cocaine papers (Freud, 1884–87) and one of his works on cerebral palsy (Freud, 1897a) have been published in translation.

*SECTION TWO*

# Description of the articles

Despite the fact that 'Aphasie' and 'Gehirn' were *dictionary* entries, they were not mere summaries of orthodox nineteenth-century neurological and aphasiological conceptions. On the contrary, the author of the articles questioned many of the cardinal orthodoxies of his time, and he arrived at some idiosyncratic and controversial conclusions.

'*Aphasie*' is much shorter than 'Gehirn'. It begins by defining the concept of aphasia. The eternally controversial questions of the psychological structure of speech and language and their localization in the cortex of the brain are then addressed. In this discussion the author states his own (very definite) opinions on the subject. That polemic is followed by a description of the various clinical aphasiological syndromes. This nosographic section includes descriptions of the so-called hysterical and neurasthenic 'aphasias'. The article ends with a brief note on therapeutic and prognostic issues.

*'Gehirn'* is one of the longest articles in Villaret's dictionary. It was intended to be an introduction to nineteenth-century knowledge of the structure and function of the human brain. The article is divided into two parts, the first on neuroanatomy and the second on neurophysiology.

The first part is divided into a number of subsections. It begins by briefly describing the embryological development of the brain. The next three subsections describe the general topography of the brain and the gross anatomy of its major subdivisions. The fifth section deals with microscopic neuroanatomy and reviews the advantages and disadvantages of the various histological techniques that were currently in use. A sixth section considers the extent to which the mysteries of brain function had yielded to neuroanatomical investigation. At this point the article becomes less objectively descriptive, and the author criticizes the then-orthodox conception of structuro-functional relationships in the human nervous system. The seventh and last anatomical subsection is devoted to the then-controversial subject of the course through the nervous system of the major sensory and motor pathways.

The second part of the article is on neurophysiology. It begins by considering the age-old question of the relationship between mind and body, and the author states his own view of this relationship. Then he speculates upon how basic mental processes might be represented in the brain. This section is followed by an equally speculative section on the physiology of the cerebral cortex. For the remainder of the article the physiology of the other major (subcortical) structures in the nervous system are discussed. In this respect particular attention is paid to structuro-functional relationships.

*SECTION THREE*

# The question of authorship

The uncertainty surrounding the authorship of 'Aphasie' and 'Gehirn' is due to the fact that the individual articles in the *Handwörterbuch* were unsigned. The intention behind this section is to establish whether or not they were, in fact, written by Freud. The following evidence will be considered: (1) documentary evidence that Freud definitely did contribute to Villaret's (1888/1891) *Handwörterbuch*; (2) citations from documents known to have been written by Freud where reference is made to the two articles; (3) the juxtaposition of statements and viewpoints expressed in the articles with comparable material in the published works of Freud; (4) a critical review of existing arguments for and against Freud's authorship of the articles.

A list of contributors appears on the title pages of both volumes of the *Handwörterbuch*. In both volumes the list contains the entry: 'Dozent Dr. *Freud* in Wien'. It can therefore be asserted with some certainty that Freud contributed at least one article to each volume of Villaret's dictionary.

This is supported by a remark that Freud made in a letter to his friend Wilhelm Fliess dated 28 May 1888:

> Such time and opportunity as there has been for work has gone on *a few articles for Villaret*. . . . [Freud, 1954, p. 56, our emphasis]

However, there is no indication in the *Handwörterbuch* itself as to who the author of each individual article was. Nor is this information available in the archival records of the publishers of the *Handwörterbuch*, Ferdinand Enke Verlag (Niendorf, personal communication, 2 December 1985).

According to the *Standard Edition* bibliography of Freud's works, he may have contributed as many as six articles to the dictionary (Strachey, 1974).[1] Translations of two of these articles were included in the *Standard Edition* ('Hysteria' and 'Hystero-epilepsy'; Freud, 1888b3, 1888b4). Apparently these two were included because of their obvious relevance for psychoanalysis and not because they were more certainly written by Freud. In fact, there is more evidence to suggest that Freud wrote 'Aphasie' and 'Gehirn' than there is for any of the other articles.

In Freud's published writings he made individual reference to only those two of the *Handwörterbuch* articles. In a letter to Fliess dated 29 August 1888, Freud wrote:

> My part in Villaret has turned out to be less substantial than expected. *The article on brain anatomy* has been severely cut; several other bad articles on neurology are not by me. [Freud, 1954, p. 59, our emphasis]

There is only one article on brain anatomy in Villaret's dictionary, and that is 'Gehirn'. It can therefore be concluded that Freud was acknowledging that he wrote 'Gehirn'. Freud does not appear to have mentioned the *Handwörterbuch* articles again for the next 37 years; then he wrote in his autobiography:

> An invitation which I received in the same year to contribute to an encyclopedia[2] of medicine led me to investigate *the theory of aphasia*. . . . The fruit of this inquiry was a

small critical and speculative book [*On Aphasia*]. [Freud, 1925, p. 18, our emphasis]

The year that Freud was referring to was 1891 (which is when the second volume of the *Handwörterbuch* and *On Aphasia* were published). It seems that by 1925 Freud had forgotten that the first volume (which contained 'Aphasie') had been published in 1888. The statement cited above is implausible as it stands. It hardly seems possible that Freud could have *begun* the investigations that led to his book *On Aphasia* as late as 1891, because the book was already at the publishers by the end of April that year (see Freud, 1954, p. 61). Furthermore, there is no article on aphasia in the second (1891) volume of the *Handwörterbuch*. It would therefore seem reasonable to conclude that Freud was referring in his autobiography to an invitation to contribute an article on aphasia to the first (1888) volume of Villaret's dictionary. 'Aphasie' is the only such article in that dictionary.

The argument that the two articles were written by Freud is strongly supported by the content of the articles themselves. For the sake of comprehensibility, content-dependent commentary on the authorship of the articles is presented in the notes to the translations of articles (part two). However, at this stage it should be noted that this evidence includes instances of very idiosyncratic terminology known to have been coined by Freud being used in the articles, and numerous examples of extremely unusual opinions known to have been held by him being expressed in them (see section seven, notes 3, 5, 8, 9, 10; section eight, notes 38, 39, 40, 41, 47, 48, 54). Also, whenever an issue that was controversial at the time was addressed by the author of the articles, he favoured the point of view that Freud is known to have endorsed (see section seven, notes 2, 4, 11; section eight, notes 42, 64). On the other hand, there are no terms used or viewpoints expressed in 'Aphasie' and 'Gehirn' that are *not* compatible with the terms and viewpoints found in Freud's signed publications. Thus, the content of the articles would seem to support the view that they were written by Freud.

In the light of the overwhelming evidence in favour of this view, it is surprising that Freud's authorship of the articles has ever been brought into question in the first place. Actually a review of the relevant commentary in the literature suggests that, despite appearances, Freud's authorship of 'Aphasie' and 'Gehirn' *has* never been directly questioned.

The two articles have been mentioned in the literature a total of nineteen times, by thirteen authors. Eleven of those thirteen authors unconditionally attributed the articles to Freud (Kris, 1950a, 1950b, 1954; Bernfeld & Cassirer-Bernfeld, 1952; Vogel, 1953; Jones, 1953; Schoenwald, 1954; Grinstein, 1956; Andersson, 1962; Amacher, 1965; Sulloway, 1979; Forrester, 1980; Silverstein, 1985).[3] Spehlmann (1953) accepted that Freud wrote 'Aphasie' but only attributed the first half of 'Gehirn' to Freud (the part on brain anatomy). This division was probably due to the fact that Freud (1954, p. 59) wrote to Fliess that the article on brain *anatomy* had been severely cut, and Spehlmann therefore did not feel justified to attribute the second half of 'Gehirn' to Freud (the part on brain *physiology*). However, Spehlmann did not produce any evidence to suggest that the second half of the article was *not* written by Freud; nor did he directly question Freud's authorship of that half. His doubt was expressed by implication only. On the other hand, there *is* evidence to suggest that both halves of the article *were* written by the same author. The arguments contained in the two parts of 'Gehirn' are compatible with each other in all respects, even with regard to highly controversial issues (see section eight, note 64).

Strachey is the only other author who seems to have doubted Freud's authorship of the articles. He listed 'Aphasie' and 'Gehirn' in his first bibliography of Freud's works but qualified their inclusion with the statement: 'unsigned, authorship uncertain' (Tyson & Strachey, 1956, p. 20). Then, in a footnote to his translation of Freud's autobiography, Strachey wrote that Freud's contributions to Villaret's dictionary were unsigned and that they are therefore 'not certainly identifiable' (in Freud, 1925d, p. 18 n. 2). However three years later, in a footnote to his translation of another paper by Freud (1897b, p. 240, n. 1), Strachey apparently overcame his earlier hesitation and unconditionally attributed 'Aphasie' to Freud. A further three years later Strachey (1966b, p. 39) returned to the view that it is not possible to be completely sure of the authorship of the Villaret articles as a whole because they were unsigned, but he acknowledged that Freud mentioned 'Gehirn' in his letters and 'Aphasie' in his autobiography. Then, in Strachey's *Standard Edition* bibliography of Freud's works, he finally labelled *all* the Villaret articles that Freud is thought to have written as 'unsigned, authorship uncertain' (Strachey, 1974, pp. 49–50). Strachey's position on the authorship of 'Aphasie' and 'Gehirn' is therefore unclear. However it is noteworthy that Strachey said that it is uncertain who wrote the articles in Villaret's dictionary whenever he spoke of *all the articles as a group* (in Freud, 1925d, p. 18 n. 2; Strachey, 1966b, p. 39, 1974, pp. 49–50; Tyson & Strachey, 1956, p. 20) but not when he spoke of *'Aphasie' alone* (in Freud, 1897b, p. 240 n. 1) and not when he spoke—by implication—of *'Aphasie' and 'Gehirn' together* (in the latter part of his 1966b, p. 39 statement). It would therefore seem reasonable to conclude that Strachey did not directly question Freud's authorship of the two articles under discussion here.

* * *

To conclude: It can confidently be asserted that Freud wrote 'Aphasie' and 'Gehirn'. This assertion is based upon four facts: (1) There is objective documentary evidence that Freud contributed to the dictionary in which the articles appeared (Villaret, 1888). (2) Freud himself acknowledged that he contributed to the dictionary (Freud, 1954) and indirectly claimed authorship of the two articles (Freud, 1925d, 1954). (3) The—often idiosyncratic—terminology used and the—often controversial—opinions expressed in the articles are consistent with terminology that Freud used and opinions he expressed in his other writings (see the notes to the translations of 'Aphasie' and 'Gehirn'). (4) There is nothing in the articles to suggest that they were *not* written by Freud, nor has any evidence to this effect been presented in the literature. Consequently, Freud's authorship of the articles is widely accepted and has never been directly questioned.

On this basis Freud's authorship of 'Aphasie' and 'Gehirn' will henceforth be assumed to have been established, and the two articles will be referred to here as Freud (1888b1) and (1888b2) respectively.

## NOTES

1. Although this bibliography appeared in the final volume of the *Standard Edition*, which was prepared and published after Strachey's death under the general editorship of Angela Richards, we have attributed it to Strachey. It is unclear to what extent Richards actually prepared the bibliography; our decision is based on the fact that, with respect to the *Handwörterbuch* articles, the 1974 bibliography is identical with Strachey's earlier Freud bibliography (Tyson & Strachey, 1956).
2. Villaret's *Handwörterbuch* has been called an 'encyclopedia' in various other contexts (Schoenwald, 1954, p. 121; Amacher, 1965, p. 58; Strachey, 1966b, p. 39; Sulloway, 1979, p. 16; Silverstein, 1985, p. 208). This is, strictly speaking, a mistranslation. A 'Handwörterbuch' is not an 'encyclopedia' but, rather, a 'concise dictionary'.
3. However, Schoenwald (1954) mentioned only 'Aphasie', and Amacher (1965) mentioned only 'Gehirn'.

*SECTION FOUR*

# Literature review

This review of the literature on 'Aphasie' and 'Gehirn' is intended to be exhaustive.

The articles were first mentioned in Kris's (1950a) introduction to the Freud–Fliess correspondence, and here Freud's authorship of the articles was recognized for the first time.

Later that same year, in a paper on the significance of the Freud–Fliess correspondence, Kris (1950b) briefly mentioned the articles again and interpolated them between Freud's planned book on neuroanatomy,[1] which Freud was apparently writing during 1887 and 1888, and his monograph *On Aphasia*.

Bernfeld and Cassirer-Bernfeld (1952) then briefly mentioned the articles in their study of Freud's life and work between 1886 and 1887.

Vogel (1953) discussed the question of their authorship in his introduction to a republication of another article from Villaret's *Handwörterbuch* (Freud, 1888b3). Vogel saw the articles as preparatory studies for *On Aphasia* (Freud, 1891b).

Spehlmann (1953) briefly reviewed the articles (but not the second half of 'Gehirn'—see above) in his book on Freud's neurological writings. He also concluded that they were preparatory studies for Freud's (1891b) book *On Aphasia*.

Jones (1953) then mentioned the two articles in the first volume of his biography of Freud. Jones argued that, contrary to Freud's assertion (Freud, 1925d, p. 18, cited above), 'Aphasie' was probably not the source of his interest in aphasia. Jones noted that Freud had lectured on the subject of aphasia as early as 1886 and that Freud wrote in *On Aphasia* (p. 66 n. 1) that the stimulus to that study was a paper written by Exner and Paneth (1887).[2]

The English translation of the Freud–Fliess correspondence appeared in 1954. The only noteworthy difference between this and the original German version (Freud, 1950a) is that the apparently accidental omission of 'Aphasie' in the German bibliography of Freud's writings was rectified in the translation.

A study by Schoenwald (1954) appeared in the same year. He argued that 'Aphasie' provided a concise introduction to the problem of aphasia and to the way in which Freud differed from his contemporaries in his conceptualization of it. Schoenwald praised 'Aphasie' very highly and concluded that Freud's later book, *On Aphasia*, merely 'fleshed out the bones of his [1888b1] article with greater anatomical and physiological detail' (p. 123). It is important to note in this regard that Schoenwald believed that *On Aphasia* was the conceptual origin of Freud's purely psychological research, and therefore of psychoanalysis.

Grinstein's (1956) bibliography of Freud's works provided the next mention of 'Aphasie' and 'Gehirn'. Here they were unconditionally attributed to Freud.

Freud's authorship of the articles was first questioned by Tyson and Strachey (1956). This was followed by a series of remarks by Strachey on the articles scattered through the

*Standard Edition* (in Freud, 1897b; Strachey 1966b, 1974). These remarks were discussed in the previous section.

Andersson, in his study of the evolution of Freud's pre-analytical views (1962), was the first to comment at any length on 'Aphasie' and 'Gehirn'. Andersson's reading of the articles in conjunction with two of Freud's other works from the period (Freud 1888b3, 1888–89) led him to three general conclusions about Freud's early psychology: (1) This psychology was identical with associationism (Andersson, 1962, pp. 67, 68, 72). Andersson acknowledged that there were also some similarities between Freud's views and Herbartian psychology but argued that during its later phases, Herbartianism was indistinguishable from associationism (ibid., p. 225). (2) Although Freud's early psychological views did not question the validity of the associationist dogma, his neurological views were incompatible with the orthodox Meynertian scheme (ibid., pp. 65, 106), and Freud may already have been under the progressive influence of John Hughlings Jackson in 1888 (ibid., pp. 70, 70 n. 3, 107). (3) Andersson concluded that Freud saw psychological events as mere epiphenomena of a truly physiological causal process (ibid., 67, 68, 106). Thus, although Freud's approach represented a later phase of development than the speculative anatomical approach of Theodor Meynert, it was still physiologically reductionistic. This, in Andersson's opinion, was in keeping with a general trend in late-nineteenth-century neuroscience away from anatomical localizationism towards a more physiological (energic) interpretation of neural and mental life (ibid., p. 69).

Amacher (1965) then discussed the articles in his monograph on Freud's neurological education and its influence on psychoanalytical theory. He did so in the context of his general argument that 'Freud made no significant departures from the neurology of his teachers' (p. 72). Amacher argued that 'Gehirn' anticipated Freud's (1950a [1895]) 'Project for a scientific psychology' in many important respects. According to him, in both works Freud followed Meynert's view of the functional organization of the nervous system. Thus, in Freud's schema, psychical phenomena were identical with material processes in the cerebral cortex, which was the middle link in a chain of reflexly organized physiological mechanisms. Amacher emphasized three points: (1) Freud did not question Meynert's anatomical theory of neural and psychical functioning (Amacher, 1965, p. 58ff); (2) Freud, like his teachers, believed that only one type of excitation is transmitted throughout the nervous system and that all this excitation originates at the peripheral endings of the afferent nerves (ibid., pp. 23, 29 n. 6); (3) Freud, like his teachers, did not conceive of mental processes as in any detail independent of physical ones (ibid., p. 17). Amacher quoted extensively from 'Gehirn' to illustrate these points. He believed that the above three assumptions were crucial in the development of psychoanalysis. His arguments have been very influential.

Sulloway (1979) and Forrester (1980) were the next to mention the two articles. They did so without comment.

Finally, Silverstein (1985) used 'Gehirn' to support his arguments that: (1) Freud did not believe that psychical processes were completely determined by physical ones but rather that mind and brain *interacted* with each other; (2) Freud saw mind as more active and independent than did his neurological teachers, and his views were not compatible with passive associationism but, rather, with Franz Brentano's intentional 'act psychology'; (3) Freud felt justified in constructing psychological models without the necessity to correlate them with specific anatomical or physiological systems (ibid., pp. 204, 209). Silverstein, furthermore, argued that the 'Gehirn' article directly anticipated the psychoanalytical concepts of conflict and defence being central in mental life and behaviour (ibid., p. 211).

Two facts emerge from this review: (1) The articles have not received much attention in the literature. Amongst the very numerous papers and books on Freud's early neuroscientific work, the origins and early development of psychoanalysis, and the relationship between psychoanalysis and neuroscience, only nineteen mention 'Aphasie' and 'Gehirn'.[3] Of these nineteen, four contain only bibliographical references to the articles (Grinstein, 1956; Tyson & Strachey, 1956; Strachey, 1974; Forrester, 1980), and ten make little more than passing reference to the articles and their authorship (Kris, 1950a, 1950b, 1954;[4] Bernfeld & Cassirer-Bernfeld, 1952; Vogel, 1953; Jones, 1953; Strachey, in Freud, 1897b, 1925d; Strachey 1966b; Sulloway, 1979).

The second fact that emerges from the literature is that the three authors who *have* discussed Freud's 'Aphasie' and 'Gehirn' at any length are in fundamental disagreement with regard to their significance (cf. Andersson, 1962; Amacher, 1965; Silverstein, 1985). Andersson (1962) has argued that the articles demonstrate that Freud was an *epiphenomenalist* with regard to the relationship between mind and brain, whereas Amacher (1965) proposed that he subscribed to the *identity theory*, and Silverstein (1985) that he was an *interactionist*. Amacher stated that *Freud made no significant departures from the orthodox neurology of Meynert and his other teachers;* whereas Silverstein and Andersson believe that *his neurology was based upon a fundamentally different approach*. Andersson's reading of 'Aphasie' and 'Gehirn' led him to suggest that Freud was under the influence of the revolutionary neurological views of Jackson at the time. Andersson asserted that Freud *did not question the validity of association psychology* in 1888 (and Amacher believed this implicitly), whereas Silverstein wrote that Freud's views were *not compatible with passive associationism* but rather with the active psychology of Brentano. Andersson stated that Freud's move away from Meynert's anatomical reductionism in the late 1880s coincided with a new *physiological reductionism*; Silverstein argued that Freud felt justified in constructing psychological models *without the necessity to correlate them with anatomy or physiology*. These areas of controversy are discussed in detail in part three.

* * *

To conclude: Although it is generally accepted that 'Aphasie' and 'Gehirn' were written by Freud, they have rarely been mentioned in the literature. Those authors who have discussed the articles at any length suggest that they may be of some significance to the Freud scholar, but there has been little consensus on the exact nature of this significance.

## *NOTES*

1. This book was never published. Masson (in Freud, 1985d, p. 16 n. 3) claims to have found the manuscript for it. However, the document that he has is entitled 'Kritische Einleitung in die Nervenpathologie', and Jones tells us that Freud drafted a manuscript with this title in January 1886 whilst he was in Paris (see Jones, 1953, p. 232). Unfortunately Masson did not lodge a copy of the manuscript with the Sigmund Freud Archives (Blum, personal communication, 11 April 1985); it has therefore not been examined by the present editors.
2. In a footnote to Freud's translation of Charcot's lectures (Freud, 1886f, p. 124 n. 1), Freud also indicated that he was already specially interested in the subject (see Strachey, 1966a, p. 19). Some remarks in his essay on 'Das Nervensystem' (Freud, 1887f, p. 191) also suggest this.
3. Even Freud neglected to mention the articles in his own (1897b) abstracts of his pre-analytical works. It has been speculated that Freud did not mention them because they were unsigned (Kris, 1950a; Strachey, in Freud, 1925d; Strachey, 1962, 1966b) and because he was unhappy with Villaret's dictionary in general, and his editing of 'Gehirn' in particular (Kris, 1950a, 1950b). Freud also omitted other works from the abstracts (Strachey, 1962, p. 226).
4. It should be noted that Kris (1954) is a translation of Kris (1950a). This effectively reduces the total number of references to 'Aphasie' and 'Gehirn' to eighteen.

*SECTION FIVE*

# Potential importance of the articles

If 'Aphasie' and 'Gehirn' are potentially important articles, this is primarily due to the fact that they were written during a crucial phase in the development of Freud's thought.

He was 32 years old at the time. He had already discovered a new neuro-histological technique (Freud, 1884b, 1884c, 1884d); he had reported morphological observations that paved the way for the neurone theory (Freud, 1882a, 1884f [1882]; cf. Brun, 1936; Jelliffe, 1937; Jones, 1953; Brazier, 1959); he had made significant contributions to neuro-anatomical knowledge (Freud, 1885d, 1886c; Freud & Darkschewitsch, 1886b); and he had established himself as one of the founders of psychopharmacology and local-anaesthesiology (Freud, 1884–87; cf. Byck, 1974). He also had an excellent reputation as a clinical neurologist (Bernfeld, 1951; Jones, 1953).

A major shift in Freud's work away from neurology towards psychology came in 1885–86, when he studied under Jean-Martin Charcot in Paris. Hysteria and hypnotism were

Charcot's chief interests at the time, and Freud's activities upon his return to Vienna demonstrate the deep impression made on him by his exposure to these subjects. In 1886 he read papers on hypnotism and hysteria and presented a case of hysteria to his senior colleagues (Freud, 1886d); he translated Charcot's most recent lectures—which were primarily on hysteria—(Freud, 1886e); he started to do a comparative study of hysterical and organic symptomatology (Freud, 1893c), and he started to treat hysterics and neurasthenics in his private practice. During 1887 Freud began to use Joseph Breuer's 'cathartic method' in the treatment of hysterical patients,[1] and he published two reviews on neurasthenia and hysteria. In 1888 Freud published two more papers on hysteria (Freud 1888b3, 1888b4) and also a translation of Hippolyte Bernheim's book on hypnotic suggestion (Freud 1888–89). In this same year he published 'Aphasie' and 'Gehirn'.

Within the next decade or so Freud wrote his most significant and his last neurological studies (Freud & Rie, 1891a; Freud, 1891b, 1897a, 1900b). During the same period he wrote his seminal psychological and psychoanalytical works: the 'Preliminary communication' (Freud, 1893a), 'The neuro-psychoses of defence' (Freud, 1894), the 'Anxiety neurosis' (Freud, 1895), the *Studies on Hysteria* (Freud, 1895), the 'Project' (Freud, 1950a [1895]), and *The Interpretation of Dreams* (Freud, 1900a).

Thus, historically speaking, *'Aphasie' and 'Gehirn' sit astride the two major periods of Freud's working life.* From this point of view they may be considered to be potentially important articles for two reasons.

First, the two articles are amongst the last neurological writings of Freud, who is now widely acknowledged to have made important contributions to neuroscience (Brun, 1936; Jelliffe, 1937; Bernfeld, 1944; Jones, 1953; Spehlmann, 1953; Riese, 1958; Brazier, 1959; Pribram, 1962; Marx, 1966, 1967; Triarhou & del Cerro, 1985). Freud's (1891b) monograph *On Aphasia* has traditionally attracted the most attention in this regard. The importance of the monograph has been recognized since the beginning of the century (Storch, 1903;

Goldstein, 1912; Thiele, 1928). Riese (1958) called it 'a rare and brilliant piece of medical thought' (p. 289). Today it is considered to be a classic and standard work in neurology (Triarhou & del Cerro, 1985). It is cited in even the most general neuropsychological textbooks (Walsh, 1978; Heilman & Valenstein, 1979; Kolb & Whishaw, 1980; Luria, 1980). It is therefore highly noteworthy that 'Aphasie' was written three years before *On Aphasia* and, more importantly perhaps, that it was his only other published work on the subject of aphasia. Previous authors have suggested that 'Aphasie' was a 'preparatory study' for Freud's book *On Aphasia* (Spehlmann, 1953; Vogel, 1953), and Schoenwald (1954) has argued that there are very substantial links between 'Aphasie' and *On Aphasia*. It therefore seems reasonable to conclude that 'Aphasie' is particularly suitable for the further evaluation of Freud's contribution to neurology in general and aphasiology in particular.

The second reason why the two *Handwörterbuch* articles may be potentially important is that they were written during the period when Freud was making his first systematic psychopathological observations and constructing his first psychological theories (see Freud, 1954). Nineteenth-century neurologists—and especially Freud's teacher, Meynert—commonly conceptualized brain and mind within a unitary theoretical framework. It has been argued by some scholars that Freud followed Meynert's teachings and that his psychoanalytical theories are therefore inseparable from his neurophysiological assumptions (Amacher, 1965, 1974; Holt, 1965). The 'Project' (Freud, 1950a [1895])—another work from the transitional phase between Freud's neurological and psychological periods—has traditionally attracted the most attention here. This is because the 'Project' contained an apparently neurophysiological model for many of Freud's cardinal psychoanalytical theories. On this basis Amacher and Holt have concluded that the psychoanalytical metapsychology is irrevocably contaminated by antiquated neurophysiological misconceptions. In this way the whole scientific status of psychoanalysis has been brought into question. This has led to controversial attempts to isolate the clinical practice of psychoanalysis from its old metapsychological base (Gill & Holzman, 1976) and to attempts to construct a new base for it (Schafer, 1976). However not all Freud scholars agree that psychoanalysis is based upon antiquated neurophysiology (Kris, 1950b, 1954; Jones, 1953; Strachey, 1966a). Kanzer (1973), and Mancia (1983) argue that the 'Project' was only *ostensibly* a neurological document, that it was really a *psychological* model that was framed in neurological *terms*. In support of this view it has been argued that Freud did not endorse Meynert's teachings but rather followed Jackson's view that neurology and psychology were mutually exclusive realms of scientific inquiry (Fullinwider, 1983; Solms & Saling, 1986). From this latter point of view psychoanalysis is considered to be a purely psychological science, to be judged on its own merits.

In view of this controversy it is highly noteworthy that 'Gehirn'—which was written seven years before the 'Project'—was Freud's only other work on the structure and function of the human brain as a whole.[2] *It should give a clear indication of exactly what Freud's neurological assumptions really were during his formative psychological years, and whether or not this early neurological conception was substantially different from his later psychological one.* It therefore seems reasonable to believe that 'Gehirn' may shed new light on the relationship between Freud's neurological assumptions and his psychoanalytical theories.

* * *

To conclude: 'Aphasie' and 'Gehirn' are situated on the watershed between Freud's neurological and psychological periods. The current interest in Freud's pre-analytical writings has centred around two other works from this transitional phase, *On Aphasia* and the 'Project'. By virtue of their historical proximity and their similarity in terms of subject matter, 'Aphasie and 'Gehirn' are particularly suitable to supplement *On Aphasia* and the 'Project', respectively, as primary source material for the scholarly evaluation of Freud's neuroscientific work and its implications for psychoanalysis. The two articles will be examined from these points of view in part three of this book.

## *NOTES*

1. A remark in a letter to Fliess of 28 December 1887 indicates that Freud was using hypnotism by that date (Freud, 1954, p. 53). In his autobiography he wrote that from the very start he made use of hypnosis in a novel way (Freud, 1925d, p. 19). Strachey (1966c, p. 65) has pointed out that Freud used Breuer's method from the beginning; this implies that Freud started using Breuer's method some time before December 1887.
2. See, however, p. 18, note 1, this volume.

*PART TWO*

# Translations

*SECTION SIX*

# Translators' notes

In what follows we have endeavoured, as far as was possible, to maintain terminological consistency with existing translations of Freud. Strachey's 1953–74 *Standard Edition* translation of Freud's psychological works, Byck's 1974 collection of Freud's *Cocaine Papers* (1884–87), Russin's 1968 translation of Freud's *Infantile Cerebral Paralysis* (1897a), and Stengel's 1953 rendition of *On Aphasia* (1891b) guided our own efforts.

We have also attempted to retain the late-nineteenth-century flavour of the articles. Towards this end we have been guided by the one neuroscientific paper by Freud that he wrote in English (Freud, 1884c) and by Sachs's translation of Meynert's classic 1884 neuropsychiatric textbook (Meynert, 1885). Thus now-obsolete terms are rendered in their old form, and the modern equivalent is noted. However, no attempt has been made to update the neuroscientific *concepts* in the articles. Such a task would require very extensive commentary, and in any case it would be naive to presume that our current concepts are definitive.

In addition to striving for historical accuracy, we have represented the German texts as exactly and literally as possible. The overly condensed format of the articles is probably due to the fact that they were 'severely cut' by Villaret, the editor of the *Handwörterbuch* in which they originally appeared (see Freud, 1954, p. 59), but it is also certainly true that Freud's later works were better written. By rendering the articles as literally as was possible, we have almost accidentally reproduced their difficult style.

These translations have been done with the serious scholar in mind. The reader is thus assured that every insertion into the original text, however insignificant, is square-bracketed, and all potentially ambiguous material appears in the notes. Remarks upon evidence of Freud's authorship of articles are also included in the notes, as are some basic cross-references and biographical and bibliographical facts.

In recent times there has been much controversy over Strachey's translation of Freud. In view of this, our rendition of a few terms requires additional comment:

### *'Grossartige Komposition'*

In 'Gehirn' (p. 56, this volume), Freud described Meynert's conception of brain structure and function as a *'grossartige Komposition'*. In *Beyond the Pleasure Principle* (Freud, 1920g), in a very similar turn of phrase, Freud remarked that Fliess's biorhythmic theories were a *'grossartige Konzeption'* (p. 45). Strachey translated this as 'large conception'. Eissler (1971, p. 170 n. 32) and Sulloway (1979, p. 402 n. 2) have complained of his translation that it does not do justice to the praise that Freud actually bestowed upon Fliess on that occasion. It was proposed that it should rather have been translated as 'magnificent conception' (Sulloway, pp. 233, 402 n.2). Ornston (1985, p. 388), on the other hand, described Freud's phrase as a playful use of academic jargon, intended to express his doubt about the validity of Fliess's theories. He suggested that it could have been translated as 'grand design' or 'fantastic conception'. We have translated *'grossartige Komposition'* (with this little controversy in mind) as 'grand composition'. Hopefully this rendition retains the ambiguity between sarcasm and praise. Nevertheless we think it is enlightening that these phrases were both used in the context of general *criticism* of Meynert's and Fliess's respective theories. Therefore *'grossartig'* can probably safely be read as 'grandiose' (for which there is, incidentally, no better German equivalent than *'grossartig'*).

### *'Ich-Bewusstseins'*

Strachey translated *'das Ich'* as 'the ego'. It has been argued that it should rather have been 'the I' (Brandt, 1961; Brull, 1975; Bettelheim, 1983; Ornston, 1985) or 'the self' (Mahler & McDevitt, 1982). We have used 'ego' to preserve the historical link with (the authorized translation of) Freud's later writings, and because there is a long tradition of this rendition of *'Ich'* in the philosophical literature (Grossman, 1986). Nevertheless it is interesting to note that in 'Gehirn' Freud used 'ego' and 'self' synonymously. He wrote that the corpus callosum enables the perception of the two halves of the body 'to appear within the unitary point of view of ego-consciousness [*Ich-Bewusstseins*] (p. 66, this volume) and that partial nerve decussations permit the two body-halves to merge 'into an individual with unitary self-consciousness [*Selbstbewusstsein*] (p. 69, this volume).

### *'Seelenthätigkeit'*

Bettelheim (1983) has argued for the retranslation of *'Seele'* as 'soul' rather than 'mind', which had been Strachey's choice. In Bettelheim's opinion 'mind' is more intellectual and cognitive than *'Seele'*, which refers to the human essence or the seat of feeling and emotion. We have rendered *'Seelenthätigkeit'* as 'mental activity' rather than 'activity of the soul' (Freud, 1888b2) (p. 62, this volume). In the *O.E.D.*

'soul' is defined (in part) as the 'spiritual part of man regarded as surviving after death' and the 'spiritual part of man considered in its moral aspect or in relation to God' (vol. X, p. 461). 'Mind' has none of these unfortunate connotations, and it is also *not* an exclusively intellectual concept. It is defined as:

> . . . the seat of a person's consciousness, thoughts, volitions and feelings; the system of cognitive and emotional phenomena and powers that constitute the subjective being of a person. . . . [*O.E.D.*, vol. VI, p. 461]

Furthermore, there is a neurological precedent for translating *'Seele'* as 'mind'. *'Seelenblindheit'* and *'Seelentaubheit'* have always been considered equivalent to 'mind blindness' and 'mind deafness', respectively. Freud was certainly aware of this usage (see Freud, 1891b). There is also a philosophical precedent (e.g. the 'mind-body' problem).

*SECTION SEVEN*

# English translation of 'Aphasie'

**Aphasia** {α priv[ative] – φάσις speech (φημί)} (Fr. *aphasie f*; Engl. *Aphasia, Aphasy*; It. *afasia f, alalia f*); synonyms: *aphemia, alalia*—word deafness, word blindness—agraphia. By [the term] aphasia, one understands the abolition or impairment of the ability to express one's thoughts through conventional signs, or to understand such signs, despite the continuance of a sufficient degree of intelligence and despite the integrity of the peripheral sensory, nervous, and muscular apparatuses that are involved in the expression or comprehension of speech. Deaf-mutism, the speechlessness of idiots, the loss of speech in coma as well as through paralysis of the tongue and lips, therefore, do not fall under the concept of a|phasia|. A|phasia| is a psychical illness, but it must be firmly grasped that it is not necessarily linked with intellectual disturbance; the latter is to be taken as a complication every time. One distinguishes between natural or emotional speech (gestural speech) and artificial or articulate speech, of which the latter succumbs to disturbances more frequently because it is acquired later.—The manifold disturbances of articulate speech (true a[phasia] as opposed to *amimia*[1]) only become comprehensible if one appreciates the following reflection on the normal course of speech: A 'word' is not a simple idea, but a complex that consists of four elements, two sensory and two motor.[2] The two sensory [elements] are: the mnemic image for the heard word (the auditory presentation) and the optical image for the seen word (in script or print). The two motor [elements] are: the movement presentation (of the speech instruments) for the spoken [word] and the movement presentation (of the right hand) for the written word. The second and fourth of these components only play a role in the educated. Speech is learned by way of hearing. Besides this, the connections that link the four elements of the word presentation with the idea of the object must be taken into consideration.—Accordingly, there are two principal types of a[phasia], motor and sensory, and four pure forms, namely, *word deafness, word blindness, motor a[aphasia] (aphemia)*, and *agraphia*. These pure forms are encountered now and then in the clinic, but complex speech disturbances in which all four aspects of the speech function have suffered to varying degrees are much more frequent.—The part of the brain in which the material of speech presentations is connected, and where disease therefore leads to speech disturbance, is the island of Reil, with its surrounding convolution, which stretches from the frontal to the temporal ends of the hemisphere as the first frontal convolution, base of the central convolutions, inferior parietal lobule, and first temporal convolution. The speech field is therefore partially situated in the depths, and partially in the borders of the Sylvian fissure.[3] It is not developed in both hemispheres, however; in most (right-handed) people it is the left, and in others (left-handers) it is the right hemisphere, which contains the speech field. There are individual areas in the speech field of the left hemisphere, the injury of which produces a pure form of aphasia. These carry the—incidentally misleading—name of centres. Their precise circumscription is impossible at present. Thus the 'centre' for motor speech capability lies in the posterior part of the first frontal convolution (Broca's area), the centre for writing capability in the posterior part of the second frontal convolution;[4] the cortical region upon the integrity of which the understanding of heard speech depends is the first temporal convolution, and the corresponding cortical region for read speech signs is the inferior parietal lobule. Remarkably, these 'centres' for speech are the most outlying districts of the speech field and border directly on the centres of other functions (the tongue and lips, the arm, hearing and sight in general) whereas lesions lying between the centres of the speech field still seem to produce complex speech disturbances. The so-called centres for speech are therefore probably merely the radiation areas of association bundles that reach the speech field from other regions.[5]—The four pure forms of a[phasia] present clinically in the following fashion:

*I. The sensory a[phasia]s*

(a) *Word deafness.* The patients no longer understand what one says to them, despite the preservation of hearing and good intelligence. To them speech sounds like a confused noise, though the vocabulary that the patients make use of themselves is unrestricted. With word deafness, however, one does nearly always find motor speech disturbance, so-called paraphasia, which consists in the patient's use of inappropriate words for expressing his thoughts without realizing it. This paraphasia can go so far that the patient's speech becomes entirely senseless and that patients are perceived as mentally disturbed.

(b) *Word blindness* ([or] preferably, writing blindness). The patients are not able to recognize the meaning of written or printed speech signs that they see very well; otherwise they have good speech ability. Therefore they cannot read (alexia) or they read with the help of a trick whereby they trace single seen, but unrecognized letters.[6] This 'blindness' sometimes applies only to syllables, while single letters are still recognized; at other times |it applies| to letters as well. Here it is not rare that numbers are still recognized. Word blindness is nearly always complicated by unilateral restriction of the visual field (hemianopsia).

## *II. The motor a|phasia|s*

(a) Actual motor *aphasia* (aphemia). This is by far the most common speech disturbance and is mostly encountered in [its] pure form. It is characterized by abolition or diminution of the vocabulary. In extreme cases the patient only has gestures, in others only individual syllables or words or even entire phrases, with which he answers everything. He is, however, very well aware of the insufficient character of these expressions and is visibly hurt by his inability to say more than his remaining stereotypical phrases. The speech remnants of the a|phasi|c frequently have the character of interjection—'Yes', 'No'—or they consist of individual syllables, 'tan–tan',[7] and senseless combinations of these, like 'akoko', 'monomentive', eventually |combined| into entire, simply constructed sentences. All this speech is correctly articulated, which strictly distinguishes a|phasia| from paralysis of the speech instruments (alalia). If the reduction of the vocabulary is not severe, it mainly affects nouns and expresses itself insofar as the patient tries to transcribe them by indicating the actions. So, e.g., instead of 'Give me my hat', he says, 'Give me that which one puts on the—'. The speech capability of an a|phasi|c fluctuates with his general condition, however, and under the influence of excitement he can frequently experience a sudden deterioration. It is to be noted further that many a|phasic|s who are unable to articulate a specific word themselves, i.e. through their own train of thought, can repeat it if it is said to them first. This depends upon which of the manifold association pathways for speech are destroyed or preserved and finds its analogy in other forms of speech disturbance.—Motor a|phasia| frequently, but not necessarily, coexists with paralysis of the right-sided extremities or with paralysis of the cerebral pathways that govern the tongue, lips, laryngeal, and pharyngeal muscles. It is common to find motor a[phasia] in the first days after a left-sided apoplectic insult [and] for as long as the entire hemisphere continues to suffer under the consequences of the insult. Usually the speech disturbance soon diminishes. In such cases it can be perceived as an indirect focal symptom.

(b) *Agraphia* can be designated as 'a[phasia] of the hand' after a fortunate expression of Charcot's. Agraphia is found comparatively rarely in pure form. If a right-sided paralysis is present, the question of the presence of agraphia is naturally left undecided. Otherwise agraphia accompanies motor a[phasia] as a rule but does not necessarily keep pace with it. It consists of the patients putting only senseless and disconnected strokes together when instructed to write. Now and then such patients can also still write properly to dictation or copy from a model, whereas they are unable to write without such a stimulus.—One must analyse the more complicated aphasic disturbances through careful investigation in such a way that one can ascertain which connections between the individual elements of the word presentation, and between these and the idea of the designated object, are preserved or interrupted.[8] Because a[phasia] is an exquisite focal symptom, any lesion that affects the speech field can give rise to it; thus, brain haemorrhages, softenings, tumours, traumatic influences, abscess, etiological factors like heart and vascular disease, syphilis, morbus Brightii, acute infectious diseases (typhus, variola), diabetes mellitus, etc., as with the other forms of brain disease, come into consideration here, without the one or the other contributing a particular causal relationship to the form of a[phasia]. The latter rather depends solely on the localization and extent of the established lesion in the speech field.—A[phasia] is not always the consequence of a material brain process; rather, neuroses like hysteria and neurasthenia may also produce aphasic disturbances. Hysterical a[phasia] is purely motor as far as it has been studied until now. However, it is characterized by its completeness or, rather, by its absolute character. It is not that the patients are restricted to the use of individual words, but that they are completely speechless, indeed voiceless; not a sound, not a cry comes about. Hysterical a[phasia] is therefore actually a 'mutism'. Writing capability is always preserved and increased, however.[9] When questioned, these patients point at their mouths, then put pen to paper and write their thoughts down with unusual rapidity and certainty.—The speech disturbance resulting from neurasthenic brain-fatigue is limited to the forgetting of individual concrete words and to the confusion of similar-sounding words in speech and is thus similar to the paraphasia that occurs in healthy people.[10]—The *prognosis* and *therapy* for aphasia is the same as that for a paralysis and is directed to the basic complaint. Under favourable circumstances all forms of aphasic disturbance are capable of improvement or compensation. If a persistent defect of speech ability remains behind, then one can attempt to ameliorate it through the re-education of the patient. Thus the word blind [patient] learns, even if laboriously, to read again, and the agraphic learns to write again. The latter can make use of the left hand to learn to write, either in mirror-writing or in normal characters.[11] Preserved intelligence is a precondition for such learning attempts.

## *EDITORS' ANNOTATIONS*

1. Loss of the power to communicate by means of gesture or non-speech signs.
2. This and the following three sentences are relevant to the determination of the authorship of this paper. They read as a précis of Freud (1891), pp. 73ff. Freud's view that the word comprises a complex of four rudimentary ideational elements can undoubtedly be attributed to Charcot, under whom Freud studied in 1885–86; cf. Freud's translation of Charcot's *Leçons sur les maladies du système nerveux* (Charcot, 1886, p. 155).
3. Freud (1891b, p. 67) identifies this same *continuous cortical area* as the 'speech field.'

4. The localization of a unitary centre for this function was never 'definitely established', but Freud later (1891b, p. 63) identified the same region in this context.
5. The important point made in the last two sentences is more fully stated in *On Aphasia* (Freud, 1891b, pp. 62–64) and restated in Freud's abstract of that work (1897b, p. 240).
6. This pseudo-reading manoeuvre is known as 'Wilbrand's sign'.
7. This was a recurrent utterance of Broca's famous (1861) patient, Leborgne. He came to be known by the name of 'Tan' by the Bicêtre hospital staff.
8. Freud's (1891b, p. 77ff) psychology of language and classification of the aphasias followed this exact scheme.
9. This claim was also made in the 'Dora' case study (Freud, 1905e [1901], p. 39) and in the 'Hysterie' article in Villaret's dictionary (Freud, 1888b3, p. 47). The more general remarks on hysterical aphasia were also restated there and again later (Freud, 1893c, pp. 163, 164, 169).
10. Freud made a very similar point in *On Aphasia* (1891b, p. 13) and again in *The Psychopathology of Everyday Life* (1901b, p. 53); (cf. Stengel, 1953, p. xiii).
11. This method was based on the traditional assumption, made in accordance with the teaching of others, that the intact right hemisphere can take over the speech function of the damaged left one in right-handed individuals. Freud did not question this teaching (see Freud & Rie, 1891a, p.126).

*SECTION EIGHT*

# English translation of 'Gehirn'

**Brain**, the (Fr. *cerveau m*; Engl. *brain*; It. *cervello, encefalo m*, *ἐγκέφαλος* (scil[icet] *μύελος* the medulla which is in the head), *cerebrum*.

## *I. ANATOMY* OF THE BRAIN*

A. DEVELOPMENT: The embryological Anlage[1] of the later complicated shape of the brain appears as three consecutive swellings of the medullary tube which are designated as the *primitive cerebral vesicles*. The definitive brain-form originates from the inequality of the growth of these primitive vesicles. The *first cerebral vesicle* undergoes the most signifi-

---

***External circumstances have not permitted this representation to be supported by the essential illustrations. This representation itself had to take this omission into consideration. [This and other such asterisked footnotes are Freud's own. Editors' annotations are in the numbered notes.]**

cant changes. Through the thickening of its lateral walls the vesicle itself becomes the *thalamus* (thalamus opticus), and its lumen becomes the *third ventricle*. In front and laterally, a new vesicle grows out on each side—the *fore-brain vesicle*—which represents the Anlage of the cerebral hemispheres in its walls and the Anlage of the *lateral ventricles* in its lumen. The fore-brain vesicle ties itself off from the primary vesicle (twixt-brain[2]). Its lumen becomes slit-like and only remains in communication with the third ventricle by means of a small opening, the future *foramen Monroi*. From thickening of the wall on the floor of the fore-brain vesicle, the *fore-brain ganglion*, caudate and lenticular nuclei, together known as the *striate body*, [or] corpus striatum, originate. Only the first ganglion juts permanently into the ventricular space; later-on the lenticular nucleus lies closely against the hemisphere wall, without linking with it. The remaining part of the fore-brain vesicle surpasses the region of the ganglion in its growth and attains powerful development forwards, backwards, and eventually also downwards. Thus, in an arch over the *'brainstem'*, the enveloping part of the fore-brain vesicle becomes the *'brain mantle'*, the surface of which folds in typical fashion to leave convolutions and sulci, towards the end of developing in a confined space. An area on the external surface, which corresponds to the ganglia contained inside and represents the centre of the hemisphere, remains behind in its growth. At first it is visible on the foetal brain as an open fossa surrounded on three sides by the mass of the hemisphere, [i.e.] the fossa Sylvii. Later the surrounding walls close over it so that only a diagonal fissure ascending posteriorly and superiorly, called the *fissura Sylvii*, is left. The roof of the second primary vesicle (*mid-brain*) forms the corpora quadrigemina, and its lumen persists as the *aquaeductus Sylvii*. The third vesicle (*hind-brain*) becomes the *medulla oblongata*, but its roof transforms itself into connective tissue so that the central canal of the Anlage is opened in this area (*fourth ventricle*). From a prior thickening of the roof in front of the opened central canal, a powerfully growing brain part originates; [this is] the *cerebellum*, which covers the fourth ventricle from above and, through its contiguity with the corpora quadrigemina, closes it off in front. At the back it remains open and accessible (transverse section of the brain).

B. GENERAL TOPOGRAPHY: For the following description of the developed brain it is presupposed that the reader has a fresh brain in front of him. The succeeding remarks will equip him to recognize the various formations that have been given particular names, and to find roughly the seat of a disease in the brain. First of all, upon examination of a fresh brain, it is noticed that certain parts of it have a pure white colouring and others a reddish-brown to reddish-grey one. This colour distinction coincides with a highly significant structural distinction between the various brain parts. This is because the *'white matter'* consists only in medullated fibres, a little interposed substance (called neuroglia), and sparse vasculature, whereas the *'grey matter'*, in addition to such fibres, contains a series of other elements, especially nerve-cells and rich vasculature. The arrangement of the two substances against each other is, in the main, entirely regular.—Further, it is unmistakable that the outer shape of the brain approximately corresponds to a cast of the cranial hollow. The brain displays an upper convexity, which fits the roof of the cranium, and a flat base, which rests on the base of the cranium. The convexity of the brain is formed solely by the hemispheres of the cerebrum, the surface of which is grey and occupied by convolutions. A deep median indentation, which contains the sickle[-shaped] process of the dura mater,[3] divides the *cerebrum* into the *paired hemispheres* and gives each hemisphere a smooth median dividing surface. From the median fissure[4] it is not possible to look into the interior of the stem parts and ventricle because a white, transverse fibre mass—which links the hemispheres with each other and covers the ganglia—lies in the depths of the fissure (the *corpus callosum*). If one cross-sections a hemisphere at the level of the white, isthmian corpus callosum, one sees that only a thin margin of it consists of grey matter (the *cerebral cortex*), whereas the nucleus of the hemisphere is white (*medullary centre* of the hemisphere.[5]).

(a) BASE OF THE BRAIN. The plastic [form] of the base of the b[rain] coincides with the shape of the base of the cranium. The anterior cranial fossa is filled out by the two medially abutting *orbital lobes*[6] of the cerebrum. The border between anterior and middle cranial fossae (the greater wings of the sphenoid bone) corresponds to the already known *Sylvian* fissure of the hemisphere. In the lateral parts of the middle cranial fossae rest the *inferior* or *temporal lobes* of the cerebrum, which end on each side in a blunt apex,[7] and between which space is left for the median formation of the brain stem, which rests above the sella turcica and the clivus. Finally, the posterior cranial fossa is filled out by the likewise paired, but fused, hemispheres of the *cerebellum*, above which, separated by a transverse dissepiment of pachymeninx,[8] [called] the *tentorium*, lie the *occipital lobes* of the cerebrum. The spinal cord, the direct continuation of which becomes the *medulla oblongata* in the median brain stem, rises through the foramen magnum into the cranial hollow.—The base of the brain accordingly displays parts of the brain mantle, namely the lower (basal) parts of the frontal and temporal lobes, as well as parts of the brain stem. A pursuance of the latter from the spinal cord upwards allows the following form-relations to be recognized: the spinal cord increases in diametral depth and breadth during its transition into[9]

(b) the MEDULLA OBLONGATA. In one area, which roughly corresponds to the transition, its anterior fissure (v. anatomy of the *Spinal Cord* [Villaret, 1891, pp. 619–631]) appears to blur; this is the area of the *decussation of the pyramids*.[10] In favourable cases one can directly observe the diagonal crossing of white fibre bundles here. Above this the anterior tracts swell into two club-shaped, white elevations, which carry the name of *pyramids* and contain the pyramidal tracts known from the anatomy of the spinal cord. Lateral to the pyramids, two more grey elevations are found, *the olives*. A cross-section through these shows that they include a beautiful, jagged grey nucleus. The further continuation of the oblongata disappears under a broad, rounded-off, four-sided mass, which consists of white transverse fibres and is known as the *pons*. To continue the study of the oblongata, one turns over the entire brain so that it presently rests on the base, flaps back the cerebellum to the front, and now views the dorsal (upper) surface of the oblongata. Conspicuous on this is [the fact] that, through divergence, the posterior median sulcus opens the lateral parts of the medulla and finally exposes the floor of the central canal. The space thus formed is called

(c) the FOURTH VENTRICLE. The places of origin of several important cranial nerves lie under its floor, partially visible from above. It has a rhomboid boundary, with front and back apexes. The front apex is called the *calamus scriptorius*. Above, the fourth ventricle is closed by the cerebellum; below, as the new roof of the central canal, the ganglion masses of the corpora quadrigemina are found, which are contiguous with the cerebellum through a thin medullary sheet [called] the *velum medullare anterius*. The floor of the fourth ventricle, [i.e.] the oblongata, continues forwards, considerably broadened, as the basis of the brain stem. A transverse cross-section through the fourth ventricle in its greatest breadth shows a clear delimitation of an upper layer of the brain stem, which is a continuation of the oblongata, from a lower one, which corresponds to the transverse ligaments of the pons.—In this area one inspects

(d) the CEREBELLUM. It consists of a middle portion, the *vermis*, and two lateral portions, the [cerebellar] *hemispheres*. Its surface is grey and deeply grooved as transverse, parallel strips run over the vermis from one hemisphere to the other. The lower surface of the vermis is hollowed out into a repository for the medulla oblongata.[11] A cross-section of the cerebellar substance vertical to the convolutional strips shows—as with the cerebrum—a thin edge of grey cortical substance and a white tract as the nucleus of each leaf-shaped convolution.[12] The entire cross-section is, therefore, reminiscent of a leaf with ramified veins. A cross-section through the greatest width of the cerebellum shows that the bulk of the organ consists of white fibres. Furthermore, each hemisphere contains a jagged grey nucleus, the *corpus dentatum*, [which is] very similar to the described olive of the spinal cord; and inside the vermis are several lumpy grey nuclei (fastigial nucleus, globose-emboliform nuclei). The cerebellum hangs from three white fibre masses, after the severance of which the brain stem can be freely viewed. The most considerable of these three white '*brachia*'[13] of the cerebellum is the middle one named the *brachium pontis*, which reaches around the oblongata and extends into the pons. Indeed, the cerebellum and pons essentially belong together and constitute a ring, which encloses the oblongata. Another brachium of the cerebellum strives forward towards the corpora quadrigemina and gives the fourth ventricle its anterior border. It carries the name *brachium conjunctivum*. The brachium conjunctivum does not constitute a link of the cerebellum with the corpora quadrigemina, but descends below the corpora quadrigemina into the depths of the brain stem. A third brachium of the cerebellum continues into the spinal cord; it carries the name *restiform body* and appears (falsely)[14] to be a direct continuation of the posterior tract of the spinal cord, the lateral divergence of which [tract] opened the central canal.—Now let us return to the base! In front of the broad white plate of the pons, two cylindrical white bodies, which diverge strongly and disappear under the temporal poles, can be seen. These are the cerebral peduncles, [or] *crura cerebri*, which consist of longitudinal fibres and which descend into the depths of the brain stem between the ganglia. On each side a flat white strip runs over the cerebral peduncles; [this is] the *tractus opticus*, which meets the tractus of the other side in a commissure and which continues forward as the rounded *nervus opticus*. Both the tracti and nervi optici together form an X, the *chiasma* nervorum opticorum. Between the chiasma and the diverging cerebral peduncles a triangular grey area remains; [this is] the *trigonum intercrurale*, which encloses the end of the central canal of the grey substance in a funnel, [called] the *infundibulum*. From the latter a glandular organ, the ***hypophysis*** or the pituitary gland, which lies embedded in a fossa in the sphenoid bone, hangs down on a stem. Two gleaming white elevations in the trigonum carry the name *corpora candicantia* (mamillaria).[15] An area on the base of the brain in front of the chiasma, the ***substantia perforata anterior***, is important as [it is] the entrance-region of the blood vessels from the ganglia of the brain stem.—Further, one finds the exit areas of the *twelve cranial nerves* on the base of the brain: I The *n[ervus] olfactorius* is embedded in a sagittal sulcus (sulcus rectus) on the orbital surface of the frontal lobe. It appears to arise out of an area on the base in front of the substantia perf[orata] anterior and carries a grey bulge on its end, [called] the ***bulbus olfactorius***, from which the olfactory nerves enter the nasal cavity through the ethmoid bone. II The *n[ervus] opticus* (v. above). It disappears under the temporal poles with the cerebral peduncles and can be followed macroscopically up to the ganglia of the region of the corpora quadrigemina (v. [section (e)] below). III The *n[ervus] oculomotorius* emerges from the trigonum intercrurale near the anterior limit of the pons. IV The *n[ervus] trochlearis* (v. [section] e below). V The *n[ervus] trigeminus* emerges from the lateral part of the pons, where it extends into the brachium pontis. VI The *n[ervus] abducens* on the posterior limit of the pons. VII The *n[ervus] facialis* with VIII the *n[ervus] acusticus* in a fossa between the posterior limit of the pons, the olive, and the cerebellum.[16] IX The *n[ervus] glossopharyngeus* becomes visible on the lateral surface of the medulla oblongata above the next, X *n[ervus] vagus*. XI The *n[ervus] accessorius*, following the previous two, originates in a longitudinal series of rootlets from the lateral surface of the medulla oblongata (v. *accessorius* [Villaret, 1888, pp. 11–12]). XII The *n[ervus] hypoglossus* emerges from the sulcus between olive and pyramids; it continues the series of efferent anterior spinal roots upwards.[17]

(e) FURTHER FORMATIONS OF THE BRAIN STEM. If one bends the cerebrum around the transverse axis, with the frontal pole downwards, one thereby exposes

—the CORPORA QUADRIGEMINA (cf. *corpus 9* [Villaret, 1888, pp. 353–355]), and their relationship to the fourth ventricle, the cerebellum, and the oblongata, which is mentioned above. The corpora quadrigemina belong to the roof of the mid-brain vesicle, the lumen of which stretches under them as the aquaeductus Sylvii. They are divided into paired superior and inferior corpora bigemina by a sulcus median and vertical to them. The IV cranial nerve, *n[ervus] trochlearis*, arises from the velum medullare anterius between them and the cerebellum. The lateral surfaces of the corpora quadrigemina as well as two small ganglia found there, the *external* and *internal geniculate bodies* (corpus geniculatum externum et internum), are covered by a part of the next ganglion, the thalamus. To view this, one must open the ventricle by removing the corpus callosum. One then sees

—the so-called CEREBRAL GANGLIA[18] or, rath[er], their free surfaces. In fact one sees, firstly, the *thalamus* and, in front of it, the *striate bodies* or preferably *caudate nuclei* (nucleus caudatus), separated from each other by a white strip [called] the *stria cornea*. Between the two thalami gapes the *third ventricle*, bridged only in one area by the so-called inter-thalamic adhesion. The posterior commissure [which is] stretched out between the two thalami in front of the corpora quadrigemina forms the posterior border of this ventricle. In the vicinity, mostly lying against the superior corpora bigemina, is the *pineal body* [or] glandula pinealis; undoubtedly in part a nervous organ. The shape and construction of the cerebral ganglia can only be discerned by [means of] cross-sections in manifold directions. It suffices to say that contained inside the thalamus are several grey masses and diverse, well-differentiated fibre bundles. The thick end of the striate body is displayed in the ventricle, but this ganglion continues backwards in the inside of the brain stem, where it terminates in an apex[19] (tail and head of the caudate nucleus). A transverse cross-section of the brain through the middle of the caudate nucleus shows that still another cerebral ganglion is included in the inside of the brain stem; [this is] the wedge-shaped lenticular nucleus, the apex of which turns inwards and the convex base outwards. It is subdivided into three segments by concentric, white medullary strips. The two medial [segments] are called the *globus pallidus* and the lateral, darker [segment is called] the *putamen*. The lenticular nucleus and caudate nucleus together actually form a single mass [called] the *fore-brain ganglion* and are also linked by scattered grey bridges. What separates them from each other is a broad, white fibre mass called the *internal capsule*, which is recognizable as the continuation of the cerebral-peduncle fibres on the one hand, and of the medullary centre of the hemisphere on the other hand. On the same traverse section one recognizes that immediately external to the lenticular nucleus—only separated by a thin medullary span (*external capsule*)—lies the grey of the Sylvian fissure, the convolutions of which carry the name of the *Island* of *Reil*. A grey mass, detached from the cortical grey here, is designated as the *claustrum*.—To view the relationships of the internal capsule with the other ganglia better, it is advisable to make a horizontal section of one hemisphere, going through the fissura Sylvii (section parallel to the base). One [then] sees the three cerebral ganglia. In fact [one sees], laterally, the lenticular nucleus, medially, the caudate nucleus, and, lying behind it, the thalamus. One also notices that the white strip of the internal capsule is composed of two sections, the front of which runs between the lenticular nucleus and caudate nucleus, and the back [of which runs] between the lenticular nucleus and thalamus. The two limbs of the internal capsule butt in an externally open angle, which is called 'the *genu*' of the internal capsule. These details naturally refer to the position of the entire fibre path, which is to be regarded as the internal capsule, and not to the direction of the individual fibres contained therein.

C. GROUPING OF THE DESCRIBED PARTS AROUND THE CENTRAL CANAL AND ITS CONTINUATION (considering a median section of the entire brain). At the bottom the central canal of the spinal cord is covered by the posterior tracts; after their culmination it runs below the cerebellum as the fourth ventricle, then under the velum medullare and the corpora quadrigemina as the aquaeductus Sylvii, and finally it opens into the third ventricle. One sees that a hollow, tubular appendage descends to the base out of the third ventricle; [this is] the *infundibulum*, the lumen of which contains the end of the primary central hollow of the nervous system. The front wall of the infundibulum merges with the chiasma nervorum opticorum. Where the infundibulum departs from the twixt-brain substance, the cross-section of a tract consisting in transverse fibres, [i.e.] the anterior commissure, is found. The front (ventral) half of the spinal cord, the oblongata, and their continuation, together with the pons, therefore belong to the floor of the primary central canal. The back [dorsal] half of the spinal cord, the cerebellum, the velum, and the corpora quadrigemina, belong to its roof.—On the median section one also views the form of the *corpus callosum*, which connects the medullary masses of the two hemispheres with each other. It begins in a sharp edge (rostrum) in front of the infundibular region[20] on the base of the brain; it rises, swiftly increasing in massiveness, then bends into the transverse course (genu of the corpus callosum), and ends at the back in a thickened bulge (splenium). Below the free end of the corpus callosum one arrives, unhindered, at the corpora quadrigemina. A broad convolution of the medial hemisphere surface, [called] the *gyrus fornicatus*, reaches around the corpus callosum. After it has covered the end of the corpus callosum, [i.e.] the splenium, it continues on the anteriorly and inferiorly bent temporal lobe of the hemisphere and carries *Ammon's horn*, [which is] formed through the rolling-up of cortical remnants, on its pole. Accordingly, this convolutional span stretches from the basal frontal end up to the temporal end of the hemisphere.—It is not yet possible to look into the lateral ventricle from the median section. This is because the camber between the genu and horizontal body of the corpus callosum is filled out by a thin lamina, the *septum pellucidum*, which represents a rudimentary remnant of the hemisphere wall broken through by the corpus callosum. At the back the septum ends in a sharp, free edge between which [edge] and the thalamus the *foramen Monroi* lies as the entrance to the lateral ventricle. One now detaches the septum from the corpus callosum and sees the ganglia of the fore-brain protruding into the lateral ventricle. But presently one also notices a medial-lying, paired, whitish tract, which ascends from the base of the brain in the region of the trigonum intercrurale, runs over the thalamus in an arch, lies against the corpus callosum, and then detaches from it again under its end-bulge to reach Ammon's horn in the temporal pole. This arched bundle is called the *fornix*. It covers the third ventricle and represents the limit where the hemisphere vesicle was originally tied off.

D. The CONVOLUTIONS and SULCI on the surface of the hemisphere have attained great clinical significance because the recognition of the unequal value of different cortical regions necessitates as precise as possible an orientation on this organ (v. *Localization* [Villaret, 1891, pp. 231–233]). The succeeding description refers to *Exner's*[21] schema. Deviations from it come about in individual brains, [but] it is questionable whether one does not attribute too much significance to such morphological alterations. Each hemisphere has a convex exterior, a flat interior (median), and a flat basal surface, and further [it has] a frontal, occipital, and temporal pole. One differentiates a frontal, parietal, occipital, and temporal lobe on it, without always being able to sharply distinguish the one from the other. On first orientation to the convex exterior of an hemisphere one looks for the

Sylvian fissure, which ascends from the lower anterior to the upper posterior surface and distinguishes the temporal lobe from the rest of the brain. If one penetrates into the depths of this fissure, one finds 3 to 4 hidden convolutions, the *Island of Reil* or the *Insula*, which are covered by the convolutional span lying against the Sylvian fissure. One now firstly looks for a sulcus, nearly always unramified, which stretches down from the upper limit of the hemisphere to the Sylvian fissure. This separates off the frontal from the parietal lobe and is called the *central sulcus* or *sulcus Rolandi*. In front of the central sulcus, therefore in the frontal lobe, lies a vertical, downward stretching convolutional span [called] the anterior central convolution.[22] However this is not delimited on the frontal end; the three transverse convolutions of the frontal brain, which are more or less sharply differentiated from each other by two transverse sulci, are able to emerge from it. Behind the central sulcus stretches a second vertical convolution, the posterior central convolution,[23] already belonging to the parietal lobe. This convolution is delimited at the back by an—incidentally quite variable—sulcus, which first of all ascends parallel to the central sulcus but then turns backwards in an arch and thus divides the parietal lobe into two parts. The part above the last-described *inter-parietal sulcus* is called the *superior parietal lobule*, and [the part] of the parietal lobe that lies below the sulcus is called the *inferior parietal lobule*. Two of the three convolutional spans of the temporal lobe emerge downwards out of the inferior parietal lobule. These are separated by a constant sulcus in the temporal lobe, which runs parallel to the Sylvian fissure and [which] is therefore called the *parallel sulcus*.[24] The third convolutional span of the temporal lobes fuses with the occipital brain, which also cannot be sharply delimited from the parietal lobe, and [which] displays constant sulci the least frequently. In *Exner's* schema two transverse occipital sulci, and therefore three consecutive occipital convolutions, are adopted. Another two designations in the inferior parietal lobule deserve mention.

That region of it which encircles the posterior end of the Sylvian fissure in a convolutional arch is called the *gyrus supra-marginalis*; and a similar arch lying around the posterior end of the parallel sulcus is called the *gyrus angularis*.—The convolutions on the basal surface deserve no special acknowledgement. On the other hand, the arrangement of the medial hemisphere-surface is interesting. The corpus callosum, as described, is surrounded by one convolution, which reaches, uninterrupted, from the basal frontal end to the temporal pole. The anterior bounding sulcus of this convolutional span follows the gyrus fornicatus, but not for its entire course; still in front of the splenium it turns upwards and reaches the limit of the hemisphere just behind the posterior central convolution of the external hemisphere surface. The strange course of the sulcus is indicated by its name, *sulcus calloso-marginalis*. Between this sulcus and the upper limit of the hemisphere remains a convolution, likewise encircling the corpus callosum, which carries on as the *medial frontal convolution*. Its back, the piece corresponding to the two central convolutions, is called the *paracentral lobule*. After the deviation of the sulcus calloso-marginalis, the gyrus fornicatus widens up to the upper limit of the hemisphere. This [extension of the gyrus], fused together with a piece of the medial surface between the sulcus calloso-marginalis and the next deep sulcus, which roughly provides a border between the parietal and occipital lobes, is quadratically bounded and [is] called the *praecuneus*. This is because the following section of cortex is wedge-shaped—*cuneus*[25]—and lies between the last-mentioned *parieto-occipital sulcus* and a deep sulcus cutting into the gyrus fornicatus. The latter sulcus corresponds to a protrusion of the hemisphere in the ventricle, the *calcar avis*, and carries the name *fissura calcarina*. Finally, one finds the continuation of the gyrus fornicatus on the medial surface of the temporal lobe, here called the *gyrus hippocampi*, set apart from the other medial temporal cortex by a longitudinal sulcus, the *sulcus occipito-temporalis*.[26]

E. THE STUDY OF THE CONSTRUCTION OF THE BRAIN strives towards giving an exhaustive description of the course of white fibre bundles and of their links with grey substances, especially with regard to the physiological significance of individual organs and regions of the b[rain]. At present this task is solved in very small part; currently it still founders on various technical difficulties, which one strives to overcome by manifold methods. All these methods are based upon two premises, which deserve express emphasis. One can name the first premise the principle of the 'continuity of nervous tissue'. It states that the functional elements of the nervous system form an uninterrupted network, so that excitations constantly travel along a nerve-fibre or cell during their course through the nervous system.[27] The second premise is the principle of isolated conduction,[28] according to which excitations may only pass from one nervous element to the other if the two nervous elements are anatomically continuous. If these two physiological premises are incorrect, then all conclusions upon which brain research presently builds would collapse. The efficiency and the limitations of the individual methods of brain anatomy are elucidated in the following survey:

1. *The cleavage method.*[29] The oldest procedure in b[rain] research is to flay hardened white substance, as the object of gross preparation, according to the direction of its fibres. Today this procedure is still indispensable for representing certain bundles of arciform course, but is otherwise useful only for purposes of demonstration because it cannot take the mentioned characteristics of the construction of the b[rain] into account.

2. *The method of dissecting in serial sections according to various definite directions (Stilling).*[30] This procedure has become indispensable to b[rain] anatomists. It facilitates a topographical knowledge of the individual white and grey masses inside the b[rain] and the pursuit of such fibres, the

directional courses of which lie within the direction of the section. It has the disadvantage of splitting up other fibre masses into small sections, the interrelationship of which in different sections is very difficult [to determine], and it proves to be unsuitable for the separation of components of a fibre-field.

3. *The method of studying secondary degeneration.*[31] This method is based on the fact that the individual parts of the nervous system are trophically dependent upon each other. If a fibre bundle is separated from the grey substance in which its fibres terminate, then not only is the function of these fibres abolished, their structure also suffers change. This is directly visible under the microscope, [where] (after appropriate staining) the fibre bundle stands out conspicuously from the intact remainder. Thus, e.g., after interruption below the cortex of the central gyri, a particular fibre-span of the internal capsule degenerates and can be pursued, as diseased, through a particular region of the cerebral peduncle, through the pons, up to the pyramids of the medulla oblongata. It is now concluded, from the images one gets according to Stilling's procedure, that the affected fibres come from the region of the central convolutions and proceed to the pyramids in the indicated way. Where a cross-section is made up of this bundle mixed with other fibres, the degeneration serves as a marker to dissect this field analytically into its various fibre bundles. It would be unjustified to infer, however, that the fibre bundle coinciding with the degeneration does not link with other grey substance along its course, for experience has taught that such degeneration processes frequently also do not stop at grey substances, but affect the elements of the grey substances and extend further with the continuation of the degenerated bundle on the other side of the substance. Secondary degeneration, therefore, permits only the indirect, not the direct, interpretation of the contiguity of fibre masses; it acquaints us not only with fibre masses, but also with the concatenation of these, [i.e. with]

the conduction pathways, and is invaluable for the latter. One can either study secondary degeneration in cases of spontaneous disease of the nervous system (*Türck*),[32] or one can give rise to the conditions for secondary degeneration by inflicting injury on the nervous systems of animals. If one selects young animals for this (*Gudden*),[33] the effects are frequently more conspicuous; the degeneration often extends across grey substances that set a limit to the disease-process in the adult animal; and the grey substances with severed afferent fibres succumb to a growth inhibition, which is known as secondary atrophy. One must, however, doubt the assertion, which reverses the inference upon which the utilization of secondary degeneration is based, that a fibre bundle is *not* contiguous with a grey substance if it does not degenerate after the severance of the same bundle. Most central fibre bundles, then, are linked to two grey substances and are to be considered as commissures between these. Every time it is to be *empirically* established which of the two grey substances has the trophic influence on the intactness of the fibre bundle. There are fibre bundles that are never found [to be] degenerated; these consist either of fibres of very short course, or of those that are trophically protected on two ends. How the direction of degeneration coincides with the direction of physiological conduction quite obviously also comes into question, but does not permit proof.

4. *The method of studying the parallel development of masses.* What is understood by this method can best be elucidated by two examples: [1.] It is known that the relative development of the cerebrum in comparison to the masses of other brain parts varies across the animal series.[34] Now comparative observation teaches that b[rain]s with more fully developed hemispheres also possess a larger pons and stronger pyramids. From this concurrence of development in the animal series [it] is concluded that the cerebral hemispheres, pons, and pyramids are closely linked anatomically. Or [2.] It is known that the lobus and tractus olfactorius are relatively under-developed in many mammals [and that] the

same animals display under-development of convolutional spans on the medial hemisphere surface and of Ammon's horn. It is therefore to be assumed that the simultaneously under-developed parts are in close anatomical contiguity with each other. Accordingly, comparisons of this kind provide clues for the assessment of the reciprocal relationships between grey substances; but nothing more than clues, the usefulness of which has to be tested through further examination.

5. *The method of utilizing asynchronous medullary sheath formation.* This youngest and virtually most fruitful method in brain anatomy was discovered in 1876 by *Flechsig.*[35] It is based upon the fact that the fibres of the central nervous system do not form medullary sheaths simultaneously, but after each other during a long time-span of foetal and extra-uterine life. At a specific period only certain fibre masses, which consist of fibres of the same origin and like course, are always medullated;[36] and with suitable treatment of the preparation (staining after *Weigert*[37] with hematoxylin, or with gold chloride after *Freud*),[38] these fibre systems stand out from all other, still unmedullated fibres. This method has the advantage that it furnishes much richer material than the utilization of secondary degeneration; it offers information on all fibre systems and provides as many different images as |there are| different stages of development. It also indicates the contiguities of fibre bundles with grey substances more directly than the above method, for medullary development regularly stops at grey substances. Unfortunately this method only displays its full value in the early developmental stages. The more the image of medullary development approaches the definitive, the less is the benefit of studying not fully medullated preparations. The method of utilizing asynchronous formation of medullary sheaths has still by no means been exhaustively applied, but its results so far have sufficed to found a new epoch in brain research.[39]

F. Now to what extent have we succeeded, with the help of the characterized methods, to achieve an idea of the construction and of the performance of the brain? Here one cannot ignore the *Meynert*ian conception of the construction of the brain; a grand composition from the contents of which individual concepts will surely remain as a series of conclusively correct facts. For *Meynert* the grey cortex of the hemispheres is the destination of all fibre systems of the central nervous system. The grey cortex is the central place that, on the one hand, receives all excitations and, on the other hand, dispatches all motor impulses. With regard to their relation to the cerebral cortex the fibre systems fall into two groups: those that link parts of the cerebral cortex with each other—association systems—and those that link the cortex with deeper-lying grey masses and, through these, with the spinal cord and the periphery—projection systems. From the association systems, one can separate off those that link symmetrical parts of the cortex—commissures, e.g. the corpus callosum. The projection systems access the cortex in two ways. One of the principal pathways of the projection systems contains the fibres for voluntary movement and conscious sensation, the other contains the fibres for reflex (unconscious) transference of stimuli. The position of the two pathways relative to each other is best viewed if one makes a transverse section through the brain stem in the region of the superior corpora bigemina. This displays three layers: the top is the grey of the corpora quadrigemina; the middle [is] the continuation of the oblongata, named the *tegmentum* of the cerebral peduncles by *Meynert*; the bottom layer is the so-c[alled] pes [pedunculi] of the cerebral peduncles, separated from the tegmentum by a pigmented grey substance, the substantia nigra Soemmeringii. Here the tegmentum contains the reflex pathway, whereas the pes of the cerebral peduncles contains the voluntary pathways. The voluntary pathway is interrupted between this transverse section and the cortical grey by the fore-brain ganglion (lenticular nucleus and caudate nucleus), which receives cerebral peduncular fibres on the one side and dispatches the fibres of the 'corona radiata' to the hemispheres on the other side. In a similar fashion the thalami are interpolated into the course of the reflex pathway. The large medullary path that breaks through the ganglia as the internal capsule contains the fibres leading to the ganglia as well as those coming from the ganglia. If, from that transverse section, one pursues the voluntary pathway backwards (towards the spine), one finds that it enters the pons, and |that| through its grey substance it links with the cerebellum. Strongly reduced, the voluntary pathway exits the pons again and reaches the pyramids in the grey substance of the spinal cord. According to *Meynert*, therefore, the voluntary pathway is twice interrupted by grey masses and thereby subdivided into three sections. The piece thereof between cortex and cerebral ganglia is called the first segment of the projection system, the middle piece between ganglia and spinal cord grey is called the second segment, and the peripheral nerves themselves, |together| with the roots leaving the spinal cord, are to be conceived of as the third segment of the projection system. (In this representation the interruption of the voluntary pathways in the pons is neglected; the cerebellum |is|, in a way, omitted from the projection system.) Further, the continual reduction that the projection system undergoes from the cortex to the periphery is noteworthy.

In essential parts this conception of the construction of the brain has been shattered since the study of medullary development (*Flechsig*) proved that the 'voluntary pathway' stretches through the internal capsule without linking with the fore-brain ganglion, and that it passes the pons in like fashion without linking with the cerebellum through its grey substance. The voluntary pathway is also much smaller than *Meynert* defined it; it only takes up a third of the transverse section of the cerebral peduncle, and it thus proves to be the *unreduced* continuation of the pyramidal bundle from the cerebral cortex and to be *exclusively* motor. With these enlightenments the justification lapses to contrast the cerebral peduncle as the voluntary pathway with the reflex pathway of the tegmentum, and to subordinate the cerebellum and the cerebral ganglia to the functional purposes of the cerebral hemispheres. The voluntary or pyramidal pathway is simply a fibre bundle between spinal cord grey and the grey of certain regions of the cerebrum. The sensory pathway is most probably in the tegmentum of the cerebral peduncles, designated as reflex by Meynert.[40]

At present, the Meynertian system of brain construction is not to be replaced by another.[41] The following remarks should suggest what is well established today: The central nervous system is to be considered as a union of grey masses, which are directly or indirectly linked with each other by fibre bundles. Amongst these, the grey of the spinal cord with its continuation in the oblongata has a special position; it is the only grey mass that has a direct relationship with the periphery and is constructed in segments corresponding to it.[42] There are, therefore, no fibre systems that by-pass the spinal cord and ascend directly to higher-lying grey substances. From the anatomy of the spinal cord it is further evident that the larger part of the medullated fibres of the spinal cord are used to link its own grey substances, and [that] only a small part are given to the subsequent conduction of impulses to other grey substances. The same applies to the latter and also to the cerebrum. The larger number of fibre bundles in the cerebrum are its own association fibres; only a small part serve association with other grey masses. If one retains the name 'projection system' for the links of the cerebrum with the spinal cord, then the number of fibres [in that system] is eclipsed by the amount in the remaining systems. The majority of fibre systems in the brain stem serve to link grey masses with each other. All fibre systems can be described as, 1 *commissures*, which link symmetrical grey substances and thereby cross the midline, 2 *association bundles*, which link individual regions of the same grey substance with each other, and 3 *conduction systems*, which connect different grey substances. Brain anatomy has firstly to separate the bundles, leaving the individual grey substances and discover their course and destination. The continuation of a bundle, in the physiological sense, can be any other bundle that leaves the same grey substance. Any bundle can therefore have a large number of 'continuations', which subsequently conduct the impulses coming from it. The wide use of secondary degeneration and physiological experiments teaches [us] about the continuation of a bundle in the narrower sense.

**G. The course of only a few of the FIBRE SYSTEMS OF THE BRAIN is known and simultaneously interpreted physiologically, namely those that can be recognized as pieces of the central course of cranial nerves or the conduction pathways of the cerebrum for voluntary movement and conscious sensation. All remaining fibre masses and the grey substances connected with them—therefore, large areas of the hemispheres, the whole cerebellum, the two ganglia of the forebrain, and the thalami—are unknown in their function and insufficiently researched in their anatomical relationships. The clinic for lesions of the brain has failed to supply information about the functions of the last-enumerated brain parts, whereas it gives willing expression to even only slight impairment of the sensory and cranial nerves as well as of the motor and sensory pathways.**

*Course of motor conductors from*[43] *the trunk and extremities.* The pyramidal bundle or the motor pathway arises from the grey of the two central convolutions and the paracentral lobule and enters the spinal cord as described—through the internal capsule, cerebral peduncle, and pons—as the pyramidal tract. In the internal capsule one finds the bundle between the thalamus opticus and the lenticular nucleus in the so-called posterior limb, in fact just behind the genu of the internal capsule. In the cerebral peduncle it takes up the middle third of the pes. On the posterior limit of the pons it emerges as the ventralmost bundle of the oblongata, outwardly as the pyramid, and roughly at the border of the oblongata against the spinal cord (area of the decussation of the pyramids) it splits into two bundles. Of these the one retains its position relative to the medullated mantle, but the other enters the lateral tract of the opposite half of the spinal cord through the jags of the decussation of the pyramids. There is every reason to assume that the pyramidal pathway does not represent the only way [that] motor impulses from the cerebrum can reach the spinal cord. The significance of the parting of the pyramidal tract is unknown. It develops its medulla and degenerates in a descending direction; it is therefore trophically dependent upon the cortex.

*The course of the sensory pathway.* The positions of the fibre bundles of the brain that one may claim for the sensory conduction pathway are reasonably known, but still not much separated. It has been shown that there are several sensory pathways, and that these are manifoldly intertwined and in several areas are often interrupted by grey masses from which numerous other bundles simultaneously leave as continuations. The sensory pathways to the cerebrum are, accordingly, *not direct, but pieces of a colligated and also reflex linkage serving conduction.* The conduction of muscular sensibility is best known. This is represented in the spinal cord by the posterior tracts, the inner division of which (Goll's tract)[44] contains the fibres for the lower extremities, and the outer division of which[45] (in the cervical medulla) [contains] the fibres for the upper extremities. The two tracts firstly end in two grey protrusions on the oblongata, *Goll*'s and *Burdach*'s nuclei;[46] of which Goll's nuclei laterally bound the opened central canal. The links of the two nuclei with higher brain-parts are reasonably analogous to each other, yet Burdach's nuclei, as the centre for the more substantial portions of the upper extremities, have wider links. Firstly, bundles that mediate the cerebellar link arise from the two nuclei of the posterior tract[47] as the 'head of the restiform body'.[48] Other bundles that arise from the nuclei cross the midline as arciform fibres and settle, in part, in the area between the two olives lying dorsal to the pyramids. This decussated continuation of the posterior tracts carries the name '*inter-olivary tract*',[49] and the decussation from which it originates is called the *superior decussation of the pyramids* or *decussation of the lemniscus*.[50] Still other fibres from the posterior tract nuclei run to the midfield of the oblongata, which, due to its intimate mixing of grey substance and fibre-bundles, is designated as the substantia reticularis and probably represents the highly important *reflex organ* of the oblongata (*Meynert's motor field*). From here onward the pathway for muscular sensibility to the cerebrum retains its position beside the midline immediately dorsal to the pyramids, so that in the entire brain stem the fibres for the musculature are to be found together, separated into two layers. The stretch of the sensory pathway through the pons and region of the corpora quadrigemina carries the name '*medial lemniscus*', but from here on a definite separation from other bundles is lacking. We only know that the sensory muscular pathway from the thalamic region, and therefore from the upper layer of the pes peduncles, reaches into the internal capsule, where it takes up the posterior third of its posterior limb, and thereupon reaches directly to the same cortical regions as those out of which the motor pyramidal pathway originates. After ablation of this part of the cortex the sensory muscular pathway degenerates downwards until the nuclei of the posterior tracts, which atrophy as well; but it also degenerates in individual sections ascending from the latter nuclei. Its medullary development takes place at intervals corresponding to its manifold segments.—As for the pathway for cutaneous sensibility, it is well established that it lies very near to the above pathway in the internal capsule, because injuries of the posterior third of the posterior limb give rise to a total unilateral sensory disturbance, which affects skin, muscles, and sense organs. The course of the sensory cutaneous pathway through the brain stem is unknown, but |it| may likewise be found in the lemniscal region. It is known that the area of this tract is still to be found in the medullated mantle of the spinal cord.[51] The analogous behaviour of the n|ervus| trigeminus indicates that sensory conduction from the skin is firstly to be sought in fibres that lie outside and against the horn, and physiological experiments require that this pathway enters directly through the grey substance into the contralateral side of the medullated mantle.

## *II. PHYSIOLOGY OF THE BRAIN*

The b[rain] is that organ which converts centripetal excitations, supplied by the sensory pathways of the spinal cord and through the gateway of the higher senses, into purposive[53] and coordinated centrifugal movement impulses. This part of brain functioning can be traced back, according to the general schema of the reflexes, to the simple causal nexus of a mechanical event. Moreover, there exists the fact, inaccessible through mechanical understanding, that simultaneously to the mechanically definable excited state of specific brain elements, specific states of consciousness, only accessible through introspection, *may* occur. The actual fact of the connection of changes in the material state of the brain with changes in the state of consciousness, even though [this fact is] mechanically incomprehensible, makes the b[rain] the organ of mental activity.[53] Even if the nature of the connection is incomprehensible to us, it is itself not lawless, and, based upon combinations between experiences of the external senses on the one hand and internal introspection on the other hand, we are able to state something about these laws. If a specific change in the material state of a specific brain element connects with a change in the state of our consciousness, then the latter is entirely specific as well; however, it is not dependent on the change in the material state alone *whether* or not this connection occurs. If the same brain element undergoes the same change in state at different times, then the corresponding mental process can be linked with it on one occasion (it can cross the threshold of consciousness), [at] another time not. For the present we are unable to formulate the ruling over the laws governing this [any] closer. We do not know whether or not the ruling only depends, apart from [depending upon] the change in the state of the considered elements, upon the simultaneous states and changes in the state of the other brain elements, or, moreover, also depends upon still something else. We only paraphrase the process in that we speak of the voluntary directing of attention or of voluntary raising [of mentation] above the threshold of consciousness. If the connection in question occurs, then it may be the sensation of prevailing needs or their satisfaction that enters into consciousness, or sensory perceptions, or ideas of external objects; each of which consists in a sum of attributes that were formed through the relationship of repeated, simultaneous perceptions by means of different senses of the same thing, or ideas of the movements of [one's] own body and of the aims to be reached through the latter. The simplest aim-presentation is the idea of the sensation of the satisfaction of a need to be reached through an imagined movement.[54] These are the elements of the psychical event that can come into consideration on their own here.[55] If a person reaches for a grape after he has seen it, then the material excitation process in the motor nerves of the arm and the head is certainly in a mechanical causal nexus with the material excitation process in the nervus opticus which preceded it, and several segments of the entire chain of material events surely lie in the b[rain]. Now the following psychical processes *may* link with the seriate excitation of the latter. The optical sensory perception of the [colour] blue, in a specific form, excites the ideas of the other attributes of the grape as well (and thereby, those of [the grape] itself). Thirst-quenching capability also belongs to these attributes [which are] combined through previous repeated, simultaneous sensory perceptions and sensations. The ideas of thirst-quenching give rise to ideas of movements through which this [thirst-quenching]—as the imagined aim—can be reached. Thus, if all segments of the chain cross the threshold of consciousness, the psychical process is shaped in its simplest form. However, it may, on the one hand, become complicated by considerations of ethical and other nature, and, on the other hand, several or even all segments of the [psychical] process can remain under the threshold of consciousness, whereby nothing needs to be changed in the form of external effects. We have no reason whatsoever to assume that any segment of the material process needs to be shaped differently depending on [whether] the sensation, perception, or idea corresponding to it enters consciousness or not. The conviction of having voluntarily executed a movement may arise if at least the idea of the aim [of the movement] has entered consciousness. (This happens most clearly when several aims have entered into competition and a conscious motive has given the ruling). So the essential criterion for voluntary movement is entirely immaterial and only accessible through internal introspection. The material process with voluntary movement is not essentially different to that of reflex movement; the former is only differentiated from the latter in that with it such material segments in the excitation process become drawn in with [the excitation of] which changes in consciousness can co-exist, and also that certain of these changes in consciousness really do take place.[56] We only have reason to assume brain elements of that kind in the cerebral cortex. In this sense we name the cerebral cortex the organ of voluntary movement and in an analogous sense we name it the organ of sensation, perception, and ideas.[57]

The individual cortical elements not simply conducting excitation are differentiated—apart from [through] manifold histological features about the significance of which still little can be said—essentially by their connection with the different centripetal and centrifugal conductors of excitation. Only the cellular elements of the so-called motor sphere of the cerebral cortex are directly linked with the latter [centrifugal conductors] (in man, gyrus centralis anterior and posterior, gyrus frontalis inferior sinister, gyrus supramarginalis and angularis). Both the so-called motor sphere and the sensory sphere [are linked] with the former [centripetal conductors] (occipital lobe for vision, temporal lobe for hearing, lobi olfactori and gyrus fornicatus with cornu Ammonis for smell, the so-called motor sphere for touch and kinaesthesis). The significance of these connections is most clearly representable, on the basis of the available experiments and pathological experiences, with regard to the sensory spheres of vision and hearing, which as such are simply named the visual sphere and the auditory sphere. The excitation-conducting pathways of the n[ervus] opticus firstly continue, after some subcortical ganglionic interpolations—which mediate unconsciously coordinated reflexes—to cellular elements of the cortex of the occipital brain. The fact that an excitation is propagated from a specific point of the retina, by way of a specific nerve-fibre, up to a specific cellular element of the cortex of the occipital brain may link, in the above-mentioned fashion, with the fact that a perception of specific optical character enters consciousness. The doctrine of the specific energy of sensory nerves[58] names this perception the specific energy of the relevant nerve-fibre, and it recognizes only quantitative and no qualitative gradations for both the material excitation process in the nerve-fibre, with its peripheral and central end-apparatuses, and for the accompanying change in consciousness. Accordingly, in the visual sphere we must assume at least as many separate sensory elements as there are qualitatively differentiable (according to locus and colour) elements of visual perceptions. Hearing is entirely analogous. Now if different cortical sensory elements are repeatedly excited simultaneously with the peripheral sensory elements belonging to them—which happens whenever the same thing, with its features, works repeatedly on our senses—then excitation-conducting pathways appear to develop between these cortical elements.[59] These pathways develop in such a way that the future excitation of the one element links with an excitation of the others as well. This happens even if the peripheral sensory nerve-endings belonging to only the one element are affected by their adequate stimulus.[60] Additionally, the pathways develop in such a way that if the same thing, with only one part of its features, perhaps with the part belonging to the sensory qualitative 'visual sense' of the perception, presents itself—

and even here the thing presents only incompletely—then the idea, not only of all the optical attributes (optical mnemic images of the thing), but also of its acoustic attributes and the mnemic images belonging to the other senses may instantly appear in consciousness. Also appearing in consciousness are the range of corresponding experiences, the ideas of the needs to be satisfied by the thing, and the movements necessary to bring about the satisfaction.[61] Consequently an essential part of the material substrate for the recognition and for the purposive use of a thing consists in excitation-conducting pathways that develop, through experience, between one and the same cortical elements as well as [between] different cortical areas, and which are named *association fibres* because they serve the *association of ideas*. The system of association fibres makes up a substantial part of the white medullary centre of the cerebral hemispheres, which, together with the cerebral cortex, forms the *brain mantle* in physiological, anatomical, and developmental–historical antithesis to the *brain stem*. Apart from the association fibres, the white medullary centre of the brain mantle is composed of the *fibres of the corona radiata*, which represent *corticopetal* and *corticofugal conductors of excitation*, the general physiological significance of which is consequently obvious, as well as of the *commissural fibres*, namely the *callosal radiation*, which links equivalent cortical elements of the two hemispheres with each other and which places experiences delivered by the senses of the two bilaterally symmetrical body-halves in the kind of relationship with each other that enables them to appear within the unitary point of view of ego consciousness.

In the brain stem—which anatomically links the parts of the central nervous system |that are| constructed according to an easily visible plan, |viz.| the brain mantle and the spinal cord—lie apparatuses, in a restricted space, that are very differently valued according to the function that they serve as well as according to the subordinate, coordinate, and preordinate relation that they stand in to each other and to other apparatuses. This suffices to explain |why| the uncertainty that, at the moment, dominates our ideas of the functions of the brain stem in general [is] rather less than the [uncertainty dominating the] special knowledge of the relationships of the individual functions to its individual, anatomically differentiable formations.—If one can designate *association* as the essential function of the brain mantle and *reflex* [as that of] the spinal cord, then the characteristic function of the brain stem is coordination. The spinal cord appears to be a reflex apparatus, particularly in so far as it contains the largest sum of those devices through which centripetally and intracentrally propagated excitation is directed back (reflected) to the peripheral movement apparatuses, i.e. to the exterior. It does this through the large ganglion cells of its grey anterior columns, and, further, it integrates a large number of the centripetal conduction pathways, between which latter and the centrifugal [conduction pathways] the intracentral links are relatively simple.—The brain stem now joins the spinal cord as an integration apparatus for centripetal excitations in that it serves as the entrance for the sensory conduction pathways for vision, hearing, and taste as well as [for] the large sensory trigeminus pathway, and also receives the sensory impressions propagated in the spinal cord. Similarly, the motor end-stations of intracentral conduction continue, as extensions of the grey anterior columns, from the spinal cord to the brain stem where they appear—even in simplified form—as nuclei of the motor cranial nerves of the oculomotorius, trochlearis, pars motrix trigemini, abducens, facialis, and hypoglossus.[62] The brain stem also still resembles the spinal cord in the simplicity of some [of its] reflex connections, but in general the movement processes mediated by the former are distinguished in that with them complicated combinations of muscles combine in orderly fashion in the interest of the uniform fulfilment of aims. Even though the spinal cord does not lack coordinating connections, these connections do not come into the foreground here as much as in the brain stem. However, the movement purposively ordered by the brain stem is differentiated from the conscious fulfilment of aims that is mediated by the brain mantle, in that it is not linked with movement presentations in the way that [cortically mediated movement] is [linked] to the association of sensory mnemic images or of ideas that are abstracted out of such [images]. Coordination by the brain stem is always and entirely executed below the threshold of consciousness.—The pure white parts of the brain stem—therefore particularly the internal capsule, pes peduncle, and pyramids, as well as the peduncles and medullary centre of the cerebellum—entirely serve the simple conduction of excitation. The nervous junctions,[63] linked among themselves by simple conductors of excitation, lie together in a restricted space here. Indeed, here entire systems of such junctions are reciprocally penetrated so that a greater presence of united conduction pathways, such as [are found] in the spinal cord, is only to be expected when a considerable portion of the conductions from the spinal cord striving for the brain mantle—and from the brain mantle [striving] for the spinal cord—are carried through the brain stem without undergoing interruption by junctions in its systems of grey masses. However, it must be described as doubtful whether the brain stem contains direct conductions of that kind at all between the brain mantle and the spinal cord.[64] One may only expect them on the way from the corona radiata, through the internal capsule, the pes peduncles, the pons, and the pyramids, to the pyramidal pathways of the spinal cord. To be sure, the fact of the [existence of an] ability to localize tactile and temperature sensations also appears to require explanation by means of the assumption of direct conductions of excitations from the periphery up to the cerebral cortex, whereas we feel no compulsion simply to imagine pathways that serve voluntary movements—in so far as the latter are coordinated. On the contrary, we must probably assume that it is an exception if a voluntary movement of the trunk and extremities takes place without the participation of unconscious coordinating apparatuses in the interest of the maintenance of body balance.—A very important conduction characteristic is impressed on the brain stem and also [on] those pathways that—interrupted by few junctions or not [interrupted] at all—pass through this part of the brain; [this characteristic is that] they are decussated, i.e. conduct from the one side of the body over to the other. Even if not in their totality, most of the brain stem's larger [fibre] masses are [decussated]—individual differences prevail here. For the motor division of the pes peduncles the region of this crossing is the decussatio pyramidum known from macroscopic anatomy, and for the sensory division [it is] Meynert's superior decussation of the pyramids.[65] Of the other decussations, in which the brain stem is very rich, let only [the following] still be mentioned here: the semi-decussation in the chiasma nerv[orum] opt[icorum], the doubtful decussation of the trochlearis, the partial dependence of the m[usculus] recutus internus on the abducens nucleus of the other side, the decussated relationship (in the lemniscus of the tegmentum) of the n[ervus] acusticus to the temporal lobe (and to the corpus geniculatum internum as well as to the inferior corpora bigemina) of the other side, the contiguity of the one cerebellar hemisphere through its brachium conjunctivum with the red tegmental nucleus and the tegmental ganglia of the other side and through its restiform body and the inferior olive (of the same or the other side?) with the cuneate funiculus and the lateral cerebellar tract[66] pathway of the opposite half of the spinal cord.[67] For the present the physiological significance of decussations is only accessible in so far as they are partial, because only such [partial decussations] are able to offer effective means for the functional coordination of the two body-halves and for the merging of the bilaterally symmetrical double-beings into an individual with unitary self-consciousness.[68] Up to the present it has also been shown that the more exactly individual decussations are researched—in man and the higher mammals—the more certainly they have proven to be partial.

*Coordination* has been designated as the characteristic function of the brain stem. Obviously the basic features of its anatomical construction are dominated by the consideration of the production of those movement coordinations that serve the maintenance of body balance and locomotion. Should the balance of the body be maintained through changes in external circumstances and with the execution of each and every volitional impulse, then this is only possible if the intensity of the movement impulses (and that of their antagonists) leading to the displacement of the centre of gravity is subjected to the influence of centripetal excitations serving orientation in space. Through each change in the position or posture of our bodies a number of sensory impressions are generated that exert an influence on the innervation of the body musculature, without them needing to lead to conscious sensory perception. The peripheral sensory surfaces that come into consideration with this are the retina, the external skin, the nerve-radiations in the tendons, muscles, and joints, and probably also the semicircular canals and the ampules of the ear labyrinths. The respective adequate stimuli [are]: light, the pressure that the skin of the supported body parts is subjected to, the tension of the skin over the joints, the traction that is exerted on the muscles through their antagonists and on the tendons through their own and antagonistic muscles, the pressure of the joint surfaces against each other, and probably the pressure and the movement of the lymphs in the membranous semicircular canals. As long as the body is totally supported, all these movements will maintain balance, so that it either is not innervated at all, or, if this still happens, an antagonistic [movement] of equal intensity to each fraction of movement is generated. Every deviation from complete support—whether this deviation is given rise to by internal or external causes—leads to a sum of corresponding sensory stimuli, the unconsciously executed final effect of which is a sum of regulating muscle innervations. Now we have reason to assume [that there are] apparatuses in the brain stem that mediate central processes leading to this final effect. Such apparatuses must receive pathways productive of those sensory excitations and stand in conducting relationship to the motor end-stations of the spinal cord. The intracentral connections between their afferent and efferent pathways will be very complicated and require many junctions. This finds expression in strong development of grey substance. Now, two anatomical systems in the brain stem certainly appear to be provided out of consideration for these requirements. One of these systems is the cerebellum with its penduncles and with the pons; the other [is] the tegmentum of the pes peduncles with the corpora quadrigemina and the thalami.

The physiological significance of the first of these systems appears to become entirely apparent in the coordination of muscle innervations mediating body balance, and yet [it appears] not to be the only device through which this coordination can be maintained. The latter emerges from [the fact] that if dogs manage to remain alive [for] a long [period of] time after complete extirpation of the cerebellum, they again attain some degree of balance in standing and running. A few pathological experiences in humans also concur with this fact. Whether the brain mantle or the tegmental ganglia substitute curatively for the cerebellum, or whether the loss of the functions of the cerebellum can be endured to some extent because—as Schiff[69] thinks—only the fixation of the spinal column and not the coordination of the musculature of the extremities is meant to depend on the cerebellum, is unfortunately unknown. Because dogs in which the cerebellum is lacking fatigue quickly and because they display a much slighter loss in agility and power in swimming than in movement on the ground, one may be tempted to interpret [the physiological significance of the cerebellum] in the latter [Schiff's] sense, or at least in [the sense] that if the cerebellum also coordinates the musculature of the extremities, this applies only in so far as the latter [coordination] is claimed for the maintenance of balance in standing and walking, and not in so far as it is [claimed] for locomotion itself.

Very typical for those species in which the cerebellum is active in coordination is the experience that the asymmetry, and not the extent of the destruction in the region of its hemispheres or peduncles, is decisive for the magnitude of the movement disorder to be observed. This especially emerges and is also best intelligible with injuries in the area of the sensory and motor connections of the cerebellar hemispheres, whether they affect the cerebellar peduncles themselves or their cerebral continuations with regard to the medulla. It must obviously be much more disturbing when one of the above-listed [connections], the sensory pathways serving orientation in space, is only unilaterally destroyed—[i.e.] where the constantly supplied excitations of the pathway of the other side then continue to have an effect without undergoing the hitherto active compensating influence [of the now-destroyed pathway]—than when one or several orientating sensory areas of the cerebellum are entirely absent. The manifold forced postures and forced positions that arise in animals after unilateral destructions in the indicated areas, and which fade into real forced movements after making symmetrical injuries, are to be considered from this point of view. I.e. in such [forced movements] with which not only the direction and form of the movement but also the impetus towards the same [movement] is forced, [the forced movements] may hardly be the result of destruction of sensory pathways of a coordination apparatus. Only unilateral destruction in the region of the motor connections of the cerebellum, which are contained in its middle peduncle,[70] give rise to a true forced movement. It appears as self-evident that with unilateral disturbances, motor orientating innervations must result in a forced posture. However, if the centripetal and central orientation apparatus is completely preserved, then the forced posture must lead to the transmission of regulating innervations that are actually normal, but [which] now—because they work asymmetrically due to faulty centrifugal conduction—may impair the posture further, and so on. In such cases forced movement impulses are therefore sent off from the coordination apparatus itself. The *rolling movements around the longitudinal axis* of the body,[71] bordering on the miraculous in their intensity and persistence—which Magendie[72] first described as a consequence of the severance of one of the cerebellar peduncles to the pons—has been interpreted in similar fashion by Schiff. These forced movements also cease if a symmetrical [injury] is added to the unilateral injury.

It has already been noted that it is unlikely that voluntary movements are mediated by the pyramidal pathways without an apparatus controlling the maintenance of body balance being simultaneously drawn into the activity. This view finds support in reflection on the anatomical relationships that the pyramidal fibres enter into in the pons, [with] its transverse fibres, and [with] the brachium pontis of the cerebellum.—The fact, noticed through introspection, that the locomotive movements initiated by single volitional impulses are continued in regular fashion, indeed are purposively adjusted to small changes in external circumstances, even if attention is completely appropriated by conscious material elsewhere, as well as the experience that rabbits are still able to hop steadily after removal of the brain mantle, leads to the assumption that in the brain stem an apparatus is available that, once activated, transmits all new impulses regulated according to temporal and intensive conditions to the muscles serving locomotion, and [to the assumption] that the regulation of these impulses is accessible to the influence of the—above-discussed—centripetal orientating impulses. We suspect the existence of such an apparatus in the system of the tegmentum of the pes peduncles with the corpora quadrigemina and the thalami. This localization of the postulated apparatus is made rather likely by the experience that rabbits, after removal of the cerebrum inclusive of the striate body and lenticular nucleus,[73] are still able to hop steadily, and [the experience] that dogs in which the cerebellum has been extirpated still run. Moreover, we know for certain that the coordination of a movement complex that is in close relationship to the regulation of locomotive (and equilibrial) innervations is mediated by that system, as is the case for coordination of eye muscle movements, without which visual impressions could not be utilized to find spatial orientation. Because of the connections of the mentioned system with the orientating sensory surfaces and with the peripheral organs of movement, anatomy does not leave us in an awkward situation. For an idea of this, we hardly have a clue [about] how the individual anatomically differentiable formations of that system participate in locomotive coordination. In this respect it only has to be emphasized that stimulation of the thalamus has no motor effect; that neither partial nor total destruction of one or both thalami gives rise to noticeable movement disturbances, and that a rabbit, however, in which one thalamus is totally destroyed and one in which this injury is effected bilaterally, lets the contralateral extremities and all extremities [respectively] get into positions that the animal first has to change considerably before it can execute a hop. One can also say that the thalami of rabbits are in close relationship to the reflex maintenance of readiness to hop during reposal. We do not know where in the brain stem the hopping movements themselves are coordinated and where, as a result of the sensory excitations that the one hop has produced, the impetus to the coordinated reflex movement of the next hop originates. However, [from the fact] that an apparatus that achieves this is available in the brain stem and that the corpus striatum is in a conspicuous—but still unexplained—relationship to this apparatus, it is evident that after ablation of the brain mantle with the striate body, or after injury to one of the latter in a restricted area,* rabbits display regular reflex paroxysmal hopping movements, which are only limited by strong resistances or, if these are lacking, by the fatigue of the animal. We do not know by means of which pathways the first impulse is sent to the postulated apparatus as soon as wilful intention focuses on locomotive movement, and [we know] just as little [about] the ways and means through which attention from the brain

*Nothnagel's[74] nodus cursorius, extremely near to the free edge of the nucleus caud[atus] [which is] turned toward the ventricle, roughly in the middle of its length; depth unknown.

mantle, when it remains turned toward locomotive movement, meshes in a special regulating manner with the mechanical activity of that apparatus. However, this much is quite well established: the fibres of the corona radiata are not appropriated for this [purpose]. Rather, these appear to conduct excitations to the brain mantle, and people have speculated that they contain the pathways along which the material for the formation of movement presentations is supplied to the cortex. This material would be composed of sensation complexes from the sense of spatial orientation, each of which [complexes] would be combined with an innervation sensation that [would] correspond to a specific combination of muscular excitations, and in fact it is these [excitations], of which movement or posture are the result, that the orientating sensation complex generates.

The tegmental system is in an important multiple relationship to the optical apparatus. The coordination of movements of the eyeball—already mentioned—results by means of the tractus opticus, the thalamus, and the oculomotor nucleus. This coordinating apparatus is also supplied with regulating excitations from orientation senses other than from the eye, perhaps by means of one of the apparatuses regulating the posture of the whole body. At the moment further details about this are not known and have still not been reconstructed through compilation of testimony about abnormal eye positions and movements (nystagmus) after different injuries in the brain stem. With regard to the coordination between the m[usculus] rectus internus of the one [side] and the m[usculus] abducens of the other side, [which is] so important for our presentation of coordination mechanisms in general, [it] is known that the excitation of the first muscle comes from the so-called abducens nucleus of the other side if it is synergic with the second muscle, that is, with conjugate lateral movement of the two eyes. With convergent movement of the eyes, in comparison, both recti interni are innervated from the oculomotorius nuclei. The same apparatus that coordinates the movement of the eyeballs thereby sets the dioptric apparatus of the eyes for near and far sight in unison, but here only the one n[ervus] oculomotorius from the oculomotor nucleus is involved. The adjustment of the width of the pupils to light stimulation and to the sensitivity of the retina also takes place in the tegmental system. In reflex pupillary contraction with light incidence as well, only nerves and centres of the brain stem are involved. However, other formations also take part in the mediation of pupillary dilation, and it is very probable that, apart from the pupillary dilating centres, which, we must assume, [are] in the tegmental system, still other central apparatuses serving pupillary dilation are interpolated along the way from here to the roots of the cervical sympatheticus ([e.g.] centrum cilio-spinale inferius).[75] The reciprocal equalization of the pupillary width of the two eyes with different strengths of light incidence is probably mediated by the commissura posterior and the ganglion habenulae. The reflex blink, the prototype of all reflexes, upon which Descartes[76] developed the concept—[which occurs] with the perception of a foreign body endangering the eyes and with stimulation of the cornea—is carried out in the tegmental system as well, with the exception of the involvement of the n[ervus] facialis.

The question, very important for the physiology of the b[rain], of whether the tegmentum with its ganglia suffices to mediate the influence of optical sensory impressions in the regulation of locomotive movement, or whether this mediation is only achieved by involvement of the cerebral cortex in mammals, can still not be conclusively answered at the moment.

Of the formations of the brain stem lying next to the brain mantle—[i.e.] of the striate body with [its] caudate and lenticular nucleus and the internal capsule—the significance of the latter [formation] is shrouded in the least mystery. It only contains conduction pathways, suggestions about the systematic subdivision of which have already been made above. The internal capsule is electrically sensitive, and one obtains defined motor results when circumscribed points of this formation are locally stimulated. This functional systematization of the white subcortical tracts, therefore, appears to continue up to the internal capsule and generally [appears] to correspond to the proven functional subdivision in the motor area of the cortex. It is, however, remarkable that the internal capsule should still remain sensitive when, after ablation of the cortical motor region, the corresponding span of the centrum semiovale has already become unexcitable through descending degeneration. Once this is established, it would indicate that motor impulses are still transmitted downwards from other points of the cortex through the fibres of the corona radiata. Conversely, the internal capsule also appears not to receive all the fibres of the corona radiata from the motor cortical region, because loss of voluntary movement only occurs after destruction of the internal capsule *and*[77] the lenticular nucleus, and [apparently] no epileptic fits are able to be triggered off by stimulation of the internal capsule. Therefore the lenticular nucleus appears to belong to the regions of origin of epileptic attacks. At the moment hardly [any] conjectures can be made about the true physiological significance that befits the interruption by ganglion cells of the lenticular nucleus, of a large part of the cortico-motor conductors. However, it must also not remain unmentioned that according to the view of one anatomist, [who is] highly regarded in this area,[78] the caudate nucleus and the lenticular nucleus (particularly its third segment) together should make up one large ganglion, the significance of which befits an independent source-region, analogous to the cortex, of downward-striving fibres, i.e. [the fibres] of the corona radiata.

A hitherto still quite unexpected fact of far-reaching implications, which appears to concern the physiology of the striate body, has been discovered in most recent times by *Aronsohn* and *Sachs*.[79] With rabbits, guinea-pigs, and dogs, a puncture—the point of insertion of which on the telencephalon is precisely reported by the discoverers—if it penetrates the brain up to the base so that it encounters the medial side of the caput corporis striate (in the vicinity of the nodus cursorius), gives rise to an increase in temperature up to that of a fever. The cortex and white matter of the fore-brain are uninvolved in the effect. There is much to be said for the view that this is not an irritation phenomenon, and by investigation of the topography of temperature, as well as by controlling the metabolism, [it] is established that increased heat *production* accounts for the greater portion of the observed increase, but [this is established] without the involvement of the apparatus regulating the *emission* of heat being excluded with certainty.[80]—Cross-sectioning of the brain stem at the lower limit of the pons is also supposed to have considerable temperature increase as a certain consequence. This temperature increase, put down to increased heat production as well, is not regarded as an irritation phenomenon, but as a consequence of the loss of moderating centres, about the position of which no details are known.

We have, hitherto, left one of the anatomically differentiable formations of the brain stem entirely untouched. Extremely special physiological significance also befits this area, delimited by anatomists as the *central cavity grey of the 4th ventricle.*[81] With the part of the brain stem dealt with up to now we essentially had to do with the coordination of the movements serving the so-called animal life,[82] and we would have placed the area to be considered presently in pure antithesis to it—i.e. [we would have] been able to leave its [the central cavity grey's] significance in the coordination of the innervations serving vegetative life as resolved—if we did not have urgent reason to assume that the coordination of *the articulatory movements for voice and speech* are [also] carried out there. Of the remaining movement complexes coordinating real vegetative [functions], which we have reason to place in close relationship to the central cavity grey of the fourth ventricle, the one that serves respiration takes first place. As far as the relationships of the medulla oblongata to the innervations of respiratory movements are concerned, we unite certain sums of ganglion cells occupying the central cavity grey of the fourth ventricle—[cells] from which excitations tetanizing the respiratory muscles are sent off—under the term *inspiratory centre* of the medulla oblongata, and in so far as the excitations in the cells making up the centre themselves originate through the reaction of the latter [cells] against their immediate environs, people call it automatic. The ganglion cells of the inspiratory centre of the medulla oblongata do not transmit the excitations directly to the inspiratory muscles, but through the mediation of motor ganglion cells of the spinal cord. However, the coordination of the inspiratory movement apparatus into regular respiratory movement is carried out neither in these cells of the spinal inspiratory muscle centres nor in their spinal connections, but [rather] in the inspiratory centre of the medulla oblongata. Now because there is also regular, active expiration, we have also come to assume an expiratory centre in the medulla oblongata that befits the coordination of expiratory muscular innervations and which can be reflexly activated. Here the most important reflex is also stimulated by the inspiratory distension of the lungs. A consequence of the latter [distension], therefore, besides the inhibition of the inspiratory centre, is the stimulation of the activity in the expiratory centre.[83] Wherever active expiration occurs in normal respiration, we may assume that it is reflexly produced in this [above] fashion, and we do not need to attribute automatism to the cells of the expiratory centre (i.e. [we don't need to attribute to these cells] the capability of functionally reacting to the condition of the immediate environs), at least not in the sense or [to the] extent that they participate in the actualization of normal respiration.—One therefore subsumes the centres for inspiration and expiration that coordinate the motor innervations for uniform exhalation under the term *the respiratory centres in the medulla oblongata*, of which the former [centre] is activated for normal automatic [inhalation] and the latter for reflex [exhalation]. This activity can be modified both reflexly or through intervention of the will. The cough, the sneeze, the sob, and the singultus[84] are reflexly modified respiratory movements. Modification of the activity of the respiratory centre [is] also called for in the coordination of other movement complexes, like in [the coordination of] those [movement-complexes] that serve speech and singing and in [the coordination of] those that make up sucking, swallowing, vomiting, eructation,[85] defecation, and pushing in birth. Because of the close relationship that all these acts have to respiration, it is probable that the coordination of the movements belonging to them is effected in the vicinity of the respiratory centre. In this sense people indeed speak of a centre in the medulla oblongata for swallowing, of one for vomiting, etc. The respiratory centre in the medulla oblongata is laid out bilaterally symmetrically; in fact, each half of the respiratory musculature responds to the affiliated side. It is true that respiration normally remains symmetrical after medial splitting of the calamus scriptorius in the midline,[86] but this symmetry disappears instantly if the vagus or trigeminus are stimulated unilaterally. The reflex thus given rise to is only displayed on the affiliated side, and once the symmetry of respiration is disturbed in this fashion, it only restores itself gradually, if at all. Intercentral connections between the respiratory centres of the two sides or semi-decussated centripetal or centrifugal fibres are therefore severed by the section.

Areas have also been discovered in the brain stem, above the medulla oblongata, through the stimulation of which respiration can be influenced. One such area with an inspiratory response to stimulation lies at the back on the floor of the third ventricle (Christiani),[87] one with an expiratory [response lies] in the environs of the front part of the aquaeductus Sylvii (Christiani), and a second inspiratory [area lies] further back between the two corpora bigemina (Martin and Booker).[88] Whether [or not] one is justified in attributing the significance of a respiratory centre to these areas is still doubtful. They may be related to the reflexes that are able to perform respiration from the higher sensory nerves.—Of the *numerous coordinations* that the central cavity grey of the fourth ventricle carries out in the service of the vegetative life, the one that concerns the circulatory apparatus occupies a special category. It deals with this [circulation] by adapting cardiac activity and vascular tonus to each other and to the prevailing needs of the whole organism and its individual parts. We have the most certain knowledge of the existence of an apparatus in the medulla oblongata, which reveals its activity in the slowing down of the heart rate by means of the n[ervus] vagus, and of one such [apparatus] that performs the innervation of the muscles constricting the blood vessels (the cardio-inhibitory and vaso-constrictive centres in the medulla oblongata). As the essential components of these centres, we again have to assume [the existence of] ganglion cells, the functional activities of which consist in the transmission of centrifugal impulses for cardio-inhibition and vaso-constriction [respectively]. The effectiveness of the regulation of these functional activities is based on the specific functional capability of [these] ganglion cells—[which are] fundamental to the centres—to react to the condition of the immediate environs (automatism), and on the anatomical disposition of the pathways that incorporate these ganglion cells as junctions (reflex). The activity of these centres is entirely deprived of the influence of the will, but not of that of the psychical affects, as they [i.e. the centres] are also affected by the state of excitation of certain parts of the cortex. [From the fact] that they are capable of 'automatic' excitation—[or] preferably 'autochthonous' [excitation] [i.e. excitation] originating on the spot [where it is found]—it is evident that a resultant increase in their activity (slowed pulse and increased blood pressure, resp[ectively]) is to be noted if the blood becomes dyspneic[89] and if intracranial pressure rises. It is not known whether this automatism also applies to the adaptation of circulatory conditions to prevailing needs according to heat emission by the skin or according to heat retention by the skin—i.e. [it is not known] whether the ganglion cells of the centres under discussion react in a purposive fashion to the temperature of their immediate environs, just like the ganglion cells of the inspiratory centre—or whether the regulation in question is carried out purely reflexly. In any case, of the very diverse regulatory reflexes, those that are mediated by the n[ervus] vagus are best apprehended. The vagus carries centripetal fibres from the lungs and from the heart to the central cavity grey of the fourth ventricle, the stimulation of which latter [fibres] produces slowed pulse, and of which former [produces] pulse acceleration. The endings of the centripetal vagus fibres in the heart are excited by an increase in intra-cardiac pressure or in the tension of the heart-wall, and the endings in the lungs are excited by inspiratory distension of the latter. In some animals (particularly in the rabbit) the vagus fibres coming from the heart are combined into a separate pathway (n[ervus] depressor) up to their entry into the laryngeus superior. Apart from—and independently of—slowed pulse, stimulation of the n[ervus] despressor results in a reduction in blood pressure. It is unknown whether the expansion of the blood vessels, [which is] fundamental to the latter [blood pressure reduction], and whether inspiratory pulse acceleration are based on reflex inhibition of the activity of the vaso-constrictive and cardio-inhibitory centres, resp[ectively], or on an increase of the activity in antagonistic centres. That such antagonistic centres exist at all is certain, but whether [they exist] in the medulla oblongata has not been determined.

A fact concerning the functions of the medulla oblongata, but the causal relationships of which are still very little apprehended, is that after unilaterally puncturing the floor of the fourth ventricle in a quite narrowly confined area (midline, back part of the front half), passing of sugar in the urine occurs. The result occurs in full strength, and the animal survives the operation best, if the puncture leaves the pons uninjured. Protracted vagus stimulation is also supposed to be able to give rise to an increase of sugar in the urine.

## *EDITORS' ANNOTATIONS*

1. I.e. primordium (see Ornston, 1985, p. 404).
2. I.e. the diencephalon.
3. I.e. the falx cerebri.
4. I.e. the inter-hemispheric fissure.
5. I.e. the centrum semiovale.
6. I.e. the orbital aspect of the frontal lobes.
7. I.e. the temporal pole.
8. I.e. dura mater.
9. This stylistic device is used throughout the present section. The sentence continues in the next paragraph.
10. I.e. the decussation of the pyramidal tracts.
11. I.e. the vellecula cerebelli.
12. I.e. the folia.
13. I.e. the cerebellar peduncles.
14. See, however, note 47 below. Freud and Darkschewitsch (1886) studied the complex connections of the restiform body; cf. Meynert (1885, p. 128), who saw it as a direct continuation of the posterior tract.
15. I.e. the mammillary bodies.
16. Freud (1886c) studied the origins of the nervus acusticus in great detail.
17. Freud (1886c) made an analogous claim for the nuclei of the nervi acusticus, glossopharyngeus, trigeminus, and vagus in relation to the posterior spinal roots.
18. I.e. the basal ganglia.
19. It is not clear what is meant here; the caudate actually terminates in the amygdala, and this was known at that time (cf. Meynert, 1885, p. 46).
20. I.e. in the region of the infundibular recess.
21. Sigmund Exner (1846–1926), under whom Freud studied in Brücke's laboratory from 1876 to 1882; Freud later included him among the figures in his early scientific life, 'whom I could respect and take as my models' (Freud, 1925d, p. 9).
22. I.e. the precentral gyrus.
23. I.e. the postcentral gyrus.
24. I.e. the superior temporal sulcus.
25. Latin for 'wedge'.
26. I.e. the collateral sulcus.
27. Cf. Freud (1950a [1895]) p. 298. Some of Freud's earliest researches (1882a, 1884f [1882]) were devoted to the investigation of this principle.

28. One of the great objections against the theory that the nerve impulse was electrical in nature was that the nerve fibre was too poorly insulated for isolated conduction to be possible (see, for example, Ludwig, 1861). This would seem to suggest that the 'excitation' referred to here is neuroelectric (cf. Strachey, 1966d).
29. The use of this method is traditionally linked with the name of Marie Bichat (1771–1802).
30. Benedict Stilling (1810–1879).
31. This method was first used by Augustus Waller (1816–1870).
32. Ludwig Türck (1810–1868).
33. Bernhard von Gudden (1824–1886); see Jones (1953, p. 210).
34. I.e. in different species.
35. Paul Flechsig (1847–1929) was Meynert's greatest rival, and Freud's interest in his work probably represented the beginning of his estrangement from Meynert (see Bernfeld, 1951, and Jones, 1953; cf. Freud's discussion of Meynert's reaction to these 'newer methods', Freud, 1925d, p. 11). The name of Flechsig appears again later in the history of psychoanalysis—as the subject of a number of Schreber's paranoid delusions (Freud, 1911).
36. I.e. myelinated.
37. Carl Weigert (1845–1904).
38. This reference to Freud's (1884b; 1884c; 1884d) technique is relevant to the question of the authorship of this paper. By 1888 it had proved to be an unreliable procedure and was not widely used (see Upson, 1888).
39. Cf. Freud (1893f, p. 15), where Flechsig's work is described in almost identical terms.
40. This last paragraph is relevant to the determination of the authorship of this paper. It is strikingly similar to the critique of Meynert's theory delivered by Freud three years later (1891, p. 48ff).
41. Cf. Freud, 1891b, p. 49, where exactly the same statement was made.
42. Cf. Freud, 1891b, p. 50, and 1897b, p. 241, where the same assertion was made.
43. This should perhaps read as 'to'; the word used in the German original was *'von'*.
44. I.e. the fasciculus gracilis.
45. I.e. the fasciculus cuneatus.
46. I.e. nucleus gracilis and nucleus cuneatus.
47. Freud and Darkschewitsch (1886) discovered this link between Burdach's nucleus and the cerebellum.
48. The use of this term, which refers to the dorsal half of the central portion of the restiform body, is relevant to the determination of

the authorship of this paper. It was coined by Freud and Darkschewitsch (1886) and was not widely used.

49. I.e. the stratum interolivare lemnisci, the complex anatomy of which was described by Freud (1885d).
50. I.e. the sensory decussation or the decussation of the medial lemniscus.
51. I.e. in the white matter of the cord.
52. The word used in the German original, '*zweckmässig*', which is here translated as 'purposive', also has connotations of expedience, appropriateness, and usefulness.
53. Silverstein (1985, p. 209) has offered an alternative translation of this and the following sentence.
54. Cf. Freud's 'Project', Part I. Section 11: 'The experience of satisfaction' (1950a [1895], p. 317f).
55. It is unclear what this sentence refers to.
56. Silverstein (1985, p. 309) has offered an alternative translation of this sentence.
57. Freud (1915e, p. 174) appears later to have disavowed the view that consciousness can be 'localized' in the cortex of the brain. However, in 1888 he still held this view (cf. Freud, 1888–89, p. 84.)
58. This is actually a statement of von Helmholtz's doctrine of the specific energy of sensory *fibres*, which was an adaptation of Müller's law of specific sensory *nerve* energies.
59. Cf. Freud's (1950a [1895], p. 300ff) theory of 'facilitation'.
60. The concept of 'adequate stimulus', which is related to the specific nerve-energy doctrine, refers to a stimulus to which a specific receptor responds effectively. Light waves, for example, are the adequate stimulus for visual receptors.
61. The last five sentences together form one sentence in the German original. In order to make the latter comprehensible, it has been translated more freely than has the rest of the article. Amacher (1965, pp. 58, 59) has offered an alternative translation of these five sentences and the next one.
62. See note 17 above.
63. In the German original this word is '*Schaltstücke*', which literally means 'switch-pieces'.
64. This, and many similar statements throughout this section, tend to contradict the belief (apparently held by Spehlmann, 1953) that the second half of this paper was not authored by Freud. In the next sentence, for instance, it will be noted that the author does not follow Meynert's conception of the course of the motor tract from the cortex to the periphery; he follows the alternative system proposed in the first half of the paper.
65. See note 50 above.

66. I.e. the dorsal spino-cerebellar tract.
67. See note 65 above (cf. Freud & Derkschewitsch, 1886).
68. I.e. unitary self awareness or ego consciousness.
69. Moritz Schiff (1823–1896); compare these statements with Meynert (1885, p. 165), who disagreed with Schiff.
70. I.e. the brachium pontis.
71. I.e. adversive movements.
72. François Magendie (1783–1855).
73. The meaning of this distinction is not clear; the lenticular nucleus is, of course, part of the striate body.
74. Carl Nothnagel (1841–1905), in whose clinic Freud worked as an *Aspirant* in 1882–83, and who later supported Freud's appointments as *Privat-Dozent* and Associate Professor.
75. I.e. the ciliary ganglion.
76. René Descartes (1596–1650) introduced the reflex concept in his *Passions de l'Ame* of 1649.
77. Translators' emphasis.
78. It is unclear who this is.
79. This is a reference to Aronsohn and Sachs (1884) or (1885–86).
80. Translators' emphases.
81. I.e. the periventricular grey.
82. I.e. 'animated' life, as opposed to the periventricular part, which essentially serves vegetative (visceral) life.
83. This is known as the Hering–Breuer reflex; it was jointly discovered in 1868 by Karl Hering and Freud's later scientific collaborator, Joseph Breuer.
84. I.e. the hiccup.
85. I.e. burping.
86. I.e. sagittal sectioning.
87. Arthur Christiani (1843–1887).
88. This appears to be a misspelt reference to Martin and Brooker (1878).
89. I.e. hypoxic.

*PART THREE*

# Exposition

*SECTION NINE*

# Introductory remarks

In part one we argued that 'Aphasie' and 'Gehirn', two relatively unknown neuroscientific articles by Sigmund Freud, are potentially important documents both from a psychoanalytical and from a neuroscientific point of view. In part two we presented our translations of 'Aphasie' and 'Gehirn'. In this third part we examine the articles in detail and attempt to estabish the nature of their significance.

This is not the first time that these two articles have been evaluated in the psychoanalytical literature. They have been discussed before, at some length, by Andersson (1962), Amacher (1965), and Silverstein (1985). Our review of this literature (in part one) revealed that these three authors were in fundamental disagreement with regard to the true nature of the significance of 'Aphasie' and 'Gehirn'. Three absolutely contradictory interpretations of the articles were given. In this part we will attempt to resolve the dispute, and we will use the previous arguments as a point of departure for our own examination of the historical and theoretical significance of the two articles.

This part is arranged according to the following plan: First, we examine the significance of 'Gehirn' for psychoanalysis. 'Gehirn' is considered before 'Aphasie' (that is, in the opposite order to that in which the translations themselves were presented) because some of the general arguments we wish to put forward in relation to 'Gehirn' have a more specific applicability in the case of 'Aphasie'. The examination of 'Gehirn' is subdivided into four sections, each addressing one controversial question that was raised by our review of the literature. Second, we examine the psychoanalytical significance of 'Aphasie' from a similar point of view. This leads us into territory not covered by the previous expositors of these texts. In the next section, the significance of 'Aphasie' for neuroscience is evaluated. Finally, we look at the neuroscientific significance of 'Gehirn'.

*SECTION TEN*

# Significance of 'Gehirn' for psychoanalysis

Freud wrote 'Gehirn' two years after he studied under Charcot in Paris, whilst he was constructing his very earliest psychological theories (see Freud, 1954). 'Gehirn' may therefore by useful in suggesting answers to the following four controversial questions: (1) What position did Freud take with respect to the conceptual relationship between mind and body during his transition into psychoanalysis? (2) Was Freud under the influence of the orthodox neurological theories of his teacher, Meynert, during this crucial period in his intellectual life? Was he under Jackson's influence? (3) Was Freud's 'Project' a neurophysiological model for psychoanalytical theory, or was it a truly psychological model framed in neurophysiological terms? (4) Which psychological school did Freud belong to when he was constructing his earliest psychological theories? Was he an associationist? Was he influenced by Herbart or Bretano?

*1*

Andersson (1962) believed that Freud endorsed the *epiphenomenalist* view of the mind–body relation. According to this view mental events are mere shadows of physical events, akin to the evanescent shadows cast by the movement of a body. It implies a strictly one-way causal relationship: the physical causes the mental, but the mental never causes the physical. It also implies that mental events are totally dispensable, that the entire course of events in the physical world would have been exactly the same, whether or not there had ever been any minds at all. The relationship can be likened to the indifferent behaviour of a body on a cloudy day when it casts no shadows. It would obviously have important implications for the scientific status of psychoanalysis if Freud conceived of mental phenomena within this philosophical framework whilst he was making his first psychological observations. For example, it would imply that the fundamental nature of dreaming can ultimately be determined by neurophysiological methods alone and that psychological theories of dreaming are subordinate to neurophysiological ones. The validity of the psychoanalytical theory of dreams has recently been questioned from precisely this point of view (McCarley & Hobson, 1977; cf. Vogel, 1978; Wasserman, 1984).

Amacher (1965) expressed a view very similar to Andersson's when he asserted that Freud did not conceive of mental processes as being in any detail independent of physical ones. Amacher believed that Freud subscribed to the so-called *identity theory*.[1] According to this theory, mental states are isomorphic with certain brain states. To say that an individual is in a certain frame of mind is to say that a certain event is occurring in the brain, that they are literally the same event. From a philosophical point of view mind–body monism is not necessarily incompatible with the notion of an independent psychological science (see Davidson, 1980). However, Amacher understood it to mean that Freud assumed the workings of the mind and those of the brain to function according to identical principles. Amacher also believed that Freud, like Meynert, thought that the brain functioned according to simple reflex principles. For this reason (according to Amacher) Freud's psychoanalytical metapsychology is based on the assumption that mental life obeys the same simple reflex laws that characterized Meynert's neurophysiology. Thus psychoanalytical metapsychology is argued to be irrevocably tied to a particular (now discredited) nineteenth-century neurophysiological theory (Holt, 1965; Amacher, 1974). This raises the question of whether or not the clinical practice of psychoanalysis can be separated from its 'contaminated' metapsychological base (Gill & Holzman, 1976).

Silverstein (1985), on the other hand, claimed that Freud's earliest writings suggest that he was an *interactionist*. Interactionists assert that physical events cause mental events and that these mental events, in their own right, cause physical events. Silverstein believed that Freud's interactionism reflected the fact that he took an *active* view of psychical life whereby the mental determinants of behaviour were considered to be no less important than their neural counterparts. Nevertheless, interactionism is probably also incompatible with the notion of an *independent* psychological science. From an interactionist point of view the broken sequences of conscious mental life are still ultimately conceptualized with reference to non-psychological causes and effects (see Freud, 1940a, p. 158).

The following sentences from 'Gehirn' go some way toward solving this problem:

> The b[rain] is that organ which converts centripetal [sensory] excitations . . . into purposive and coordinated centrifugal movement impulses. *This part* of brain functioning can be traced back, according to the general schema of the reflexes, to the simple causal nexus of a mechanical event. Moreover, there exists the fact, *inaccessible through mechanical understanding*, that simultaneously to the mechanically definable excited state of specific brain elements, specific states of consciousness,

> only accessible through introspection, may occur. [p. 62, this volume; our emphasis]

This and other statements in the article (e.g. see pp. 63, 64, this volume) decisively refute Amacher's argument that Freud was an identity theorist. It is clear that Freud did *not* believe that the internal structure of mental processes can be reductively explained in terms of reflex brain events.

Silverstein quoted the following in support of his view that Freud (1888b2) conceived of the relationship between mind and body in interactive terms:

> . . . the essential criterion for voluntary movement is entirely immaterial and only accessible through internal introspection. The material process with voluntary movement is not essentially different to that of reflex movement; the former is only differentiated from the latter in that with it such material segments in the excitation process become drawn in with [the excitation of] which changes in consciousness can co-exist, and also that certain of these changes in consciousness really do take place. [p. 64, this volume]

Here Freud went on to say that the material segments that are accompanied by consciousness are probably in the cerebral cortex. Although this quotation does demonstrate that Freud believed that certain psychical phenomena (i.e. intentionality) cannot be reduced to physical terms, it is not an interactionist *psycho-physical* statement. It seems to simply be a statement of the fact that certain brain elements subserve consciousness whilst others do not and that these two classes of *physical* elements interact. There is no suggestion that the conscious side of the process exerts an active influence upon the physical side; on the contrary, this statement would appear to support an *epiphenomenalist* interpretation.

Andersson's argument for this (epiphenomenalist) interpretation is difficult to repudiate. In support of his view he referred the reader to this remark by Freud (1888b2):

> We have no reason whatsoever to assume that any segment of the material process needs to be shaped differently

> depending on [whether] the sensation, perception, or idea corresponding to it enters consciousness or not. [p. 64, this volume]

Seen in isolation, this would certainly seem to prove that Freud was an epiphenomenalist in 1888. However, other remarks scattered throughout the article make it clear that (even in 1888) Freud did not conceive of 'conscious' and 'mental' as being synonymous; this gives the above citation a radically different meaning. It does not mean that Freud believed that the mental is a mere shadow of a purely physiological chain, but rather that it is causally irrelevant whether the sensations, perceptions, or ideas concomitant to physical events become *conscious* or not. Freud believed in 1888 that consciousness was a mere epiphenomenon of *unconscious mental processes*. The following two quotations clearly demonstrate this point:

> If the same brain element undergoes the same change in state at different times, then the corresponding *mental* process can be linked with it on one occasion (it can cross the threshold of consciousness), [at] another time not. [p. 62, this volume; our emphasis]

> . . . if all segments of the chain cross the threshold of consciousness, the psychical process is shaped in its simplest form. However, it may, on the one hand, become complicated by considerations of ethical and other nature, and, on the other hand, several or even all segments of the [*psychical*] process can remain under the threshold of consciousness whereby nothing needs to be changed in the form of external effects. [pp. 63, 64, this volume]

The latter quotation demonstrates not only that Freud postulated a mental unconscious as early as 1888, but also that he already conceived of its role in mental life in *dynamic* terms. The following statement lends further support to this view:

> The conviction of having voluntarily executed a movement may arise if at least the idea of the aim |of the

movement] has entered consciousness. (This happens most clearly when several aims have entered into competition and a conscious motive has given the ruling). [p. 64, this volume]

*So Freud introduced the dynamic unconscious into his work approximately seven years before the date traditionally given* (cf. Strachey, 1957a). This certainly makes 'Gehirn' an important document in the history of psychoanalysis.

To return to the original question, however, we must conclude that Freud was neither an identity theorist nor an epiphenomenalist. This is very important, because it means that there is no *a priori* reason to believe that his earliest psychological observations were contaminated by any neurological assumptions. Freud was also not an interactionist in 1888.

What view *did* Freud take of the mind–body relationship at that time? All the statements quoted above suggest that he was a dualist of some sort, probably a *psycho-physical parallelist*—a view that he openly endorsed in 1891 (see Solms & Saling, 1986).[2] The parallelist sees the mental and the physical as two absolutely independent domains, each with their own causality. Jackson was a parallelist. In a paper that Freud is known to have read (Stengel, 1963), Jackson wrote:

> Now, I speak of the relation of consciousness to nervous states. The doctrine I hold is this: first, that states of consciousness (or, synonymously, states of mind) are utterly different from nervous states; second, that the two things occur together—that for every mental state there is a correlative nervous state; third, that, although the two things occur in parallelism, there is no interference of one from the other. This may be called the doctrine of Concomitance. Thus, in the case of visual perception, there is an unbroken physical circuit, complete reflex action, from sensory periphery through highest centres back to muscular periphery. The visual image, a purely mental state, occurs in parallelism with—*arises during* (not *from*)—the activities of the two highest links of this purely physical

chain; so to speak it 'stands outside' those links. [Jackson, 1884, p. 72]

Jackson's doctrine of comcomitance freed psychology and neurology from each other. Meynert's conception, on the other hand, was characterized by unrestrained shifting between the two disciplines. In the next section we consider concrete evidence from 'Gehirn' to suggest whether Freud was a Meynertian or Jacksonian neurologist during his transition into psychoanalysis. For now, it is important to emphasize that from the philosophical point of view *Freud did not conceive of mental life as being in any way reducible to neurophysical principles when he was constructing his first psychological theories.*

## 2

Meynert was an anatomist with a tendency to broad speculation. He constructed a comprehensive theory of the functional organization of the brain and the mind almost entirely on the basis of *anatomical* considerations.

In his anatomical conception the cerebral cortex was seen as the point of origin and termination of *all* the fibres of the nervous system. Thus he compared the brain to a complicated protoplasmic organism with millions of tentacles and claws. In this analogy the body of the organism is the cortex, its tentacles are the sensory nerves, and its claws the motor nerves. Accordingly, each nerve fibre was considered by Meynert to retain its individual identity between the body-periphery and the cortex, and these nerves were subdivided into those that convey *voluntary movement and conscious sensation* between cortex and periphery, and those that subserve *reflex* movement and sensation. In terms of this anatomical model Meynert presumed that the body-periphery was projected onto the cortex in a very direct way by means of all the nerves terminating in the cortex ('projection fibres'). Meynert further assumed that every sensory impression (including sensation of movement) at the peripheral end of a fibre leaves a memory image in the cortical cell at the other end of the fibre. As a result of this the millions of images derived from each sensory modality tend to be *localized* in discreet cortical areas (i.e. the areas corresponding to the termination of the different sensory nerves), and the motor images are similarly localized in the area corresponding to the cortical origin of the motor tract. These cortical images are associated with each other by means of the 'association fibres' that connect them. Furthermore, any future excitation of a cortical cell is equivalent to the experience of a simple idea (representing the memory localized in that cell), and this idea will be associated with others in accordance with the laws of association psychology. The excitation process terminates in reflex motor discharge. Thus the cortex is the seat of all psychical phenomena, and these phenomena are the middle link in a chain of reflexly organized physiological mechanisms. This theory has deservedly been described as 'cortico-centric' (Freud, 1891b, p. 46).

Not one aspect of Meynert's anatomical model has withstood empirical investigation, and today it is derisively called 'brain mythology' (Holt, 1965). Did Freud follow this model?

In 'Gehirn' Freud asked the following rhetorical question: To what extent has neuroanatomy been able to elucidate the functional organization of the human brain? He replied that one could not ignore the Meynertian conception here, and then he proceeded to summarize that conception. Having done this, however, he immediately subjected it to a devastating critique. Freud's unambiguous view was that 'in essential parts this [Meynertian] conception of the construction of the brain *has been shattered*' (p. 57, this volume; our emphasis).

Freud's arguments against Meynert were primarily anatomical (which is appropriate in view of the fact that Meynert's 'psychology' was based almost entirely on his anatomical theory). First, Freud presented evidence that had accumulated against Meynert's 'cortico-centric' notion that the brain was constructed according to a simple sensory-motor reflex plan. He pointed out that there was no direct link between the cortex and the afferent periphery and no anatomical justification to subordinate the subcortical ganglia to the functional purposes of the cerebral cortex. He concluded that the relationship between cortex and subcortex and between brain and periphery is far more complex than Meynert believed. In this respect Freud's view had much in common with Jackson's.

Jackson introduced the doctrine of evolution to the study of the nervous system. This enabled him to conceptualize the brain as a hierarchy, the structure of which reflects its phylogenetic development. In terms of this idea Jackson asserted that the highest (phylogenetically youngest) nervous structures functioned in a more loosely organized and more voluntary way than the lower (older) nervous arrangements, which gradually come to be rigidly organized and automatic in their functions. Thus the lowest subcortical structures were viewed by Jackson as having rigidly organized, unconscious, reflex functions that gradually blend into more flexible, conscious, and voluntary functions in the highest cortical structures. He believed that the cortex and subcortex are richly interconnected and that the functions of the one are conceptually inseparable from the functions of the other.

In 'Gehirn' Freud proposed a new anatomical scheme to replace Meynert's 'cortico-centric' one. The central concept behind this scheme was that:

> The central nervous system is to be considered as a union of grey masses, which are directly or indirectly linked with *each other* [as opposed to the periphery] by fibre bundles. [p. 58, this volume; our emphasis]

In this scheme cortex and subcortex were argued to be richly interconnected (p. 58, this volume). Freud assigned a far more active role to subcortical systems, and by far the largest part of 'Gehirn' was devoted to the elucidation of the functions of those systems (pp. 66ff., this volume).

Freud (1888b2) also drew attention to new findings, which contradicted another aspect of Meynert's model. Meynert subdivided nervous pathways into 'voluntary' and 'reflex' components. Freud concluded that there was no justification to contrast the ('voluntary') crura cerebri with the ('reflex') tegmentum, as Meynert had done. In Freud's alternative scheme *he carefully avoided the temptation to define physical systems in psychological terms*; he remained upon purely anatomical ground (cf. pp. 57, 58 this volume). In this respect, too, Freud's views were compatible with Jackson's. The reader will recall that Jackson—a psycho-physical parallelist—believed that psychological concepts were 'utterly different' from physical concepts. The (Meynertian) notion that a certain anatomical pathway was exclusively reserved for voluntary activity was as utterly unacceptable to Freud as it was to Jackson.

In sharp contrast to Meynert's, Freud's theory of the anatomy of the brain was cautious and empirical. Freud was able to admit that the functional organization of the human brain was still largely unknown and that apart from a few elementary nerves and cell groups:

> All remaining fibre masses and the grey substances connected with them—therefore, large areas of the hemispheres, the whole cerebellum, the two [basal] ganglia of the fore-brain, and the thalami—are unknown in their function and insufficiently researched in their anatomical relationships. [p. 59, this volume]

We have thus gone some way towards answering the question whether Freud was a Meynertian or Jacksonian neurologist during his transition into psychoanalysis; but what does all this mean for psychoanalysis? (1) It is obvious that *Freud certainly did not slavishly follow the neurology of his teachers,*[3] *and therefore psychoanalysis cannot be criticized with indiscriminate reference to their neurological misconceptions.* (2) *Freud's negation of the physiological supremacy of the cerebral cortex paved the way for his challenge to the dominance of consciousness in mental life*. Meynert believed that all psychological phenomena (conscious phenomena) occurred in the cortex and that the cortex was the ultimate origin and destination of all other anatomical and physiological systems. Freud assigned a far more active and independent role to the subcortical systems (which were purely physiological, and therefore 'unconscious', in Meynert's scheme). By thus deflating the functional importance of the cerebral cortex, Freud was able to assign a more modest role to consciousness. (3) *The idea that subcortical structures have important integrating functions of their own permitted Freud to conceptualize psychical phenomena independently of their physical base*. We have argued this point elsewhere (Solms & Saling, 1986). We know that in Meynert's scheme the whole psychological field was confined to the activities of the cerebral cortex. Cortical (mental) phenomena were thought to be activated by afferent subcortical (physical) excitations. These excitations were believed to cathect mnemic images (localized in cortical cells), which were then associated with each other—in accordance with the laws of association psychology—to produce complex ideation. In this scheme unconscious ideas were weak and inactive. *In such a scheme the psychical unconscious could only be conceived of as those latent mnemic images that at any particular point in time are not drawn into the prevailing associative network*. Once Freud had become familiar with the psychical phenomena of hysteria and hypnosis, however, it must have become obvious to him that unconscious ideas are anything but weak and inactive.

It was just as obvious to Freud as it was to Meynert and everybody else that conscious events are determined by something non-conscious. However, where Meynert claimed that they were determined by afferent *physiological* processes, Freud submitted that they were determined by powerful unconscious *mental* processes. This gave him a closed causal system, which permitted him to conceptualize mental life independently of its physical substrate. Many years later he wrote:

> Whereas the psychology of consciousness never went beyond the broken sequences which were obviously dependent upon something else, the other view, which held that the psychical is unconscious in itself, enabled psychology to take its place as a natural science like any other. [Freud, 1940a, p. 158]

Such a notion was inconceivable within Meynert's corticocentric scheme, where consciousness was directly determined by afferent physical processes. However, the neurological view that Freud first expressed in 'Gehirn' made the notion of a powerful, psychological unconscious physiologically tenable. According to this view subcortical ganglia have important integrating functions of their own and thus greatly complicate the relationship between conscious (cortical) and sensory/motor (peripheral) phenomena. This is why Freud so emphatically refused to see the cerebral cortex as the sole executive centre of the nervous system and 'to subordinate the . . . [subcortical] ganglia to the functional purposes of the cerebral hemispheres' (Freud, 1888b2) (pp. 57, 58, this volume). In Freud's decidedly Jacksonian alternative to Meynert's scheme, powerful unconscious mental phenomena could be seen as the psychological concomitants of the functions of lower (phylogenetically older) nervous arrangements. It seems that the independent mental science of psychoanalysis grew out of this scheme.

## *3*

Our reading of 'Gehirn' suggests that psychoanalysis was not moulded within Meynert's neuroanatomical scheme, as has so often been argued on the basis of material contained in Freud's 'Project'. Does 'Gehirn' throw any other new light on these previous interpretations of the 'Project'?

We wish to introduce two issues here. The first has to do with Johannes Müller's *specific nerve energy doctrine*, which Meynert rejected and which Amacher (1965) believed Freud also rejected in the 'Project'. We intend to question whether Freud did, in fact, reject the doctrine, and we intend to show that this issue has important implications for psychoanalysis. The second issue has to do with Freud's use of the concepts of *energy* and *inhibition*. How Freud used these concepts in the 'Project' has been a central question in the controversy over whether the 'Project' is a neurophysiological or a psychological model (cf. Holt, 1965; Mancia, 1983). This controversy has important implications for the scientific status of the psychoanalytical metapsychology. We intend to compare and contrast the use of these concepts in 'Gehirn' and the 'Project' in the light of this debate.

### *The specific energy doctrine*

Müller believed that there are five different types of sensory nerve in the human nervous system. These types were considered by him to represent the five senses.[4] The Law of Specific Nerve Energies, to which Müller gave systematic expression in 1838, was based upon that belief. The central and fundamental principle of the doctrine is the notion that one is never directly aware of external objects, but, rather, of the sensations in one's nerves that represent them. Nerves are thus conceived of as intermediaries between the mind and the external world and can reasonably be assumed to impose their own characteristics upon mental perception. The principle of specificity is an extension of this assumption; it states that the five different types of sensory nerve each impose their own specific energy upon the mind. Thus the doctrine asserts that if the same stimulus is applied to the different nerves, it will evoke the five different sensations appropriate to those different nerves (i.e. the specific energies of the nerves). Conversely, it asserts that if five different stimuli are applied to a single sensory nerve, they will all evoke the same sensation (i.e. the sensation specific to that nerve). This is held to be true for a stimulus applied anywhere along the whole length of the nerve.

(It is important to note that *Müller used the word 'energy' where we would use the word 'quality' today*. This is because 'energy' only acquired quantitative connotations after Hermann von Helmholtz's formulation of the theory of the conservation of energy in 1847; see Boring, 1929.)

In 1860 von Helmholtz converted the Law of Specific *Nerve* Energies into the Law of Specific *Fibre* Energies. The new doctrine was first formulated with regard to vision. It proposed that the optic nerve can be subdivided into three distinct sets of nerve fibres and that stimulation of the different fibres in these three subdivisions evokes sensations of red, green, and blue, respectively. Three years later von Helmholtz extended the theory to the auditory sense. He now proposed that the 4,500 known outer arch fibres in the ear each represents one of 4,500 different tonal qualities. By the time Freud wrote the *Handwörterbuch* articles, Müller's and von Helmholtz's theories were no longer distinguished, and the two doctrines were thought of as one.

Now, Meynert was not in agreement with these views. He wrote:

> We need not . . . accept Joh. Müller's opinion, that, at the very outset, different parts of the brain display different functional energies. A single functional energy only . . . is inherent in the brain-cell, and that is *Sensitiveness*. Actual *sensation* is developed by the evolution of . . . external forces, which we must suppose differ very materially from one another. [Meynert, 1885, pp. 138–139]

Meynert argued that the qualities of consciousness are determined not by a central neural process, but, rather, by qualitative variations in *external* energies. This was directly related to his other major physiological assumption that there are no intrinsic neural energies, that the brain obtains all its energy from the external world. According to this theory, external energies enter the organism via its peripheral afferent nerves and are discharged back into the outside world through motor activity. Within the nervous system the energy is qualitatively uniform. This physiological model complemented Meynert's anatomical model and enabled him to maintain that the nervous system is a passive, reflexly organized machine.

As is now well known, Amacher (1965) believed that Meynert's physiological assumptions were implicit in Freud's early theorizing and that they have greatly influenced psychoanalysis. This is illustrated in the following statement by Amacher—where he claimed priority over Dorer (1932) for this 'discovery':

> Dorer mentioned the fact that Meynert and Freud thought of the brain as a reflex mechanism (pp. 21, 23, 56, 105). She did not, however, mention that this idea, as held by Meynert and Freud, involved the conception that all the excitation at work in the nervous system was of one type and that all this excitation originated at the afferent periphery of the nervous system. *It was this variation of the reflex concept, rather than simply the reflex concept itself, which was crucial in the development of Freud's theories.* [Amacher, 1965, p. 29 n. 6]

Holt (1965) expanded upon this aspect of Amacher's work. He argued that Freud unhesitatingly adopted Meynert's 'passive reflex model' as a set of necessary starting points in his own thinking and that psychoanalytical theory still incorporates these same assumptions. He then listed five facts from modern neurophysiology which decisively refute and contradict the model: (1) The nervous system is active; neurones periodically fire and their non-transmitted activity waxes and wanes *without external stimulation*. (2) The effect of external stimulation is to *modulate* pre-existing neural activity; *it merely imposes order and patterning on it*. (3) The nervous system does not *transfer* energy; *the nerve impulse is propagated*. (4) *Neural energies are qualitatively different from impinging external stimuli*; the sensory nervous periphery is not a conductor but a transducer. (5) The nerve impulse bears coded *information*, not quotas of energy; *nerve energies are quantitatively negligible*. Holt concluded that, because psychoanalysis still incorporates Meynert's misconceptions about the nature of the nerve impulse, it is full of 'obscurities, fallacies and internal contradictions' (ibid., p. 109). This was held to apply especially to the economic point of view.

Later Amacher (1974) took this argument even further and claimed that the idea of a sexual aetiology in the neuroses, the wish-fulfilment theory of dreams, the notions of infantile erogenous zones and phases of psychosexual development, and the pleasure principle were all based upon this Meynertian misconception. This is because Freud is alleged to have fitted his clinical findings into Meynert's 'hydraulic reflex' model (Amacher, 1974, p. 221; see also Amacher, 1965, p. 73).

These arguments (especially with respect to the economic point of view and the pleasure principle) have subsequently come to enjoy wide acceptance. Obviously all of this is of great importance to psychoanalysis. For this reason the following statement in 'Gehirn' is of considerable interest:

> The fact that an excitation is propagated from a specific point of the retina, by way of a specific nerve-fibre, up to a specific cellular element of the cortex of the occipital brain may link . . . with the fact that a perception of specific optical character enters consciousness. *The doctrine of the specific energy of sensory nerves* names this perception the specific energy of the relevant nerve-fibre. . . . Accordingly, in the visual sphere we must assume at least as many separate sensory elements as there are qualitatively differentiable (according to locus and colour) elements of visual perceptions. Hearing is entirely analogous. [p. 65, this volume; our emphasis]

It seems that Freud endorsed not only Müller's theory of qualitatively specific nerve energies, but also von Helmholtz's elaboration of the theory—the doctrine of specific fibre energies. Therefore those aspects of Amacher's and Holt's conclusions that were based upon the view that Freud conceptualized nervous transmission in purely quantitative terms are unfounded, at least when applied to 'Gehirn'. Do they hold true for the 'Project', the primary source for their arguments?

In the 'Project' Freud proposed that a certain class of neurones (system $\omega$) react not to quantities of nervous excitations but, rather, to a patterned, *qualitative* aspect of those excitations (viz. the 'period' of their excitation). There Freud wrote:

> Where do these differences of period spring from? Everything points to the sense organs, whose qualities seem to be represented precisely by different periods of neuronal motion. The sense organs act not only as Q-screens, like all nerve-ending apparatuses, but also as sieves; for they allow the stimulus through from only certain processes with a particular period. They then probably transfer this [*qualitative*] difference to $\phi$, by communicating to the neuronal motion periods which differ in some analogous way (*specific energy*); and it is these modifications which proceed through $\phi$ via $\psi$ to $\omega$, and there, where they are almost devoid of quantity, generate conscious sensations of qualities. [1950a [1895], p. 310, our emphasis]

So, in the 'Project', too, Freud endorsed the doctrine of qualitatively specific nerve energies. Nevertheless, the 'Project' model is not *entirely* incompatible with Meynert's scheme. The relationship between environmental energies and the systems $\phi$ and $\psi$, for example, was consistent with parts of that scheme. But here we must remember that the 'Project' was only one amongst many in a series of working drafts that Freud composed over a period of two years. Furthermore, the 1895 'Project' is the one draft that he disowned as an 'aberration'. The draft that is believed to have inspired Chapter Seven of *The Interpretation of Dreams*, on the other hand, was based on Freud's January 1896 revision of the 'Project' (see Solms & Saling, 1986). In this 1896 version the systems $\phi$ and $\psi$ were assigned radically different functions:

> The nerve-paths which start from terminal organs do not conduct *quantity* but their particular *qualitative* characteristic [i.e. their specific energy]. They add nothing to the

sum [of quantity] in the $\psi$-neurones, but merely put these neurones into a state of excitation. . . . In my new scheme I insert . . . [the] perceptual neurones ($\omega$) between the $\phi$-neurones and the $\psi$-neurones; so that $\phi$ transfers its quality to $\omega$, and $\omega$ transfers neither quality nor quantity to $\psi$, but merely excites $\psi$—that is, indicates the direction to be taken by the free . . . [$\psi$] energy. [Freud, 1954, p. 142, our emphasis]

This theory is purged of all traces of Meynert's sensory-motor, hydraulic reflex model. Energies from the external world have absolutely no quantitative effect upon the nervous system; *all quantitative excitations are endogenous.*[5] In *The Interpretation of Dreams*—which was a major source of Freud's later theorizing—this revised model was retained (the system $\omega$ was now renamed the system Pcpt-Cs):[6]

But what part is there left to be played in our scheme by consciousness, which was once so omnipotent and hid all else from view? Only that of *a sense organ for the perception of psychical qualities*. In accordance with the ideas underlying our attempt at a schematic picture, we can only regard conscious perception as the function proper to a particular system; and for this the abbreviation Cs. seems appropriate. In its mechanical properties we regard this system as resembling the perceptual systems Pcpt.; as being *susceptible to excitation by qualities*. . . . Excitatory material flows in to the Cs. sense-organ from two directions: from the Pcpt. system, whose excitation [is] *determined by qualities* . . . and from the interior of the apparatus itself, whose quantitative processes are *felt qualitatively* in the pleasure–unpleasure series. [Freud, 1900a, pp. 615, 616, our emphasis]

The extent to which this delicate psychological scheme enabled Freud to transcend Meynert's mechanical sensory-motor reflex model is evident in the following passage:

The qualitative excitation of the Pcpt. system acts as a regulator of the discharge of the mobile quantity in the psychical apparatus. We can attribute the same function to the overlying sense-organ of the Cs. system. By perceiving new qualities, it makes a new contribution to directing the mobile quantities of cathexis and distributing them in an expedient fashion. By the help of its perception of pleasure and unpleasure it influences the discharge of the cathexes within what is otherwise an unconscious apparatus operating by means of the displacement of quantities. It seems probable that in the first instance the unpleasure principle regulates the displacement of cathexes automatically. But it is quite possible that consciousness of these qualities may introduce in addition a second and more discriminating regulation, which is even able to oppose the former one, and which perfects the efficiency of the apparatus by enabling it, in contradiction to its original plan, to cathect and work over even what is associated with the release of unpleasure. We learn from the psychology of the neuroses that these processes of regulation carried out by the *qualitative* excitation of the sense organs play a great part in the functional activity of the apparatus. [Freud, 1900a, pp. 616, 617, our emphasis]

There can be no doubt that *at the time that Freud was developing his fundamental psychoanalytical concepts, he had a model almost directly antithetical to the passive, hydraulic reflex model in mind.*[7] Thus on the basis of something written in 'Gehirn' (i.e. Freud's endorsement of the specific energy doctrine) we have been able to reinterpret important aspects of the 'Project' and *The Interpretation of Dreams* and thereby dismantle an influential argument against aspects of the psychoanalytical metapsychology. *There seems to be little justification for the belief that any aspect of the metapsychology was founded upon the orthodox neurological assumptions of his teachers.*

(This should be seen in conjunction with our previous conclusion that in terms of the philosophical framework within which Freud was working, psychology was independent of *any* neurological considerations.) The important question of whether Freud's 'quantities' were psychological or physiological will now be addressed.

### *The concepts of energy and inhibition*

Kanzer (1973) was one of the first to opine that the 'Project' was really a set of *psychological* propositions drawn from clinical observation but clad in neurophysiological terms. He based this conclusion upon a careful reading of that document in relation to the writings of Freud that immediately preceded and followed it. Mancia (1983) reached the same conclusion, but he based it upon an examination of the 'Project' in relation to the *neurophysiological* work of its period. He argued that in two crucial respects Freud did not take cognisance of existing neurophysiological knowledge when he wrote the ostensibly neurophysiological 'Project': (1) Mancia pointed out that by 1895 it had already been established that the nerve impulse is propagated as a wave of depolarization without physical transfer or accumulation of energy (cf. Holt, 1965, above). Nevertheless, in Freud's 'Project' a whole range of psychical processes were explained in terms of the physical transfer and accumulation of energy ($Q\dot{\eta}$) between and within ideas (neurones). (2) Mancia argued that the concept of the central inhibitory action of certain neural elements had also been established by 1895. Nevertheless, no inhibitory elements were postulated in the 'Project'. Instead, inhibition was conceived of in terms of lateral deviations (side-cathexes) of energy. Thus, according to Mancia, two basic concepts in the 'Project' were conceived independently of available neurophysiological knowledge, even though they were clad in neurophysiological terms. He concluded that the terms 'energy' and 'inhibition' were really vehicles for truly psychological concepts. This conclusion was grounded upon the *assumption* that Freud was familiar with the advanced concepts of propagated nerve depolarization and central inhibitory neural elements.

In this respect 'Gehirn' is a valuable source of evidence. It is an unquestionably neuroscientific paper in which Freud expressed his opinions on a wide range of anatomical and physiological subjects. We have already seen that in it he did not hesitate to admit the limitations of physical explanatory concepts when applied to psychical questions. It is therefore unlikely that he concealed psychological propositions in neurological terms (or vice-versa, for that matter) in this article.

A careful reading of 'Gehirn' from this point of view suggests that Mancia may have been right. *Freud's conception of nervous transmission in 'Gehirn' and his energy transfer concept in the 'Project' appear to refer to fundamentally different processes.* The notion, central to the 'Project', that quotas of energy can occupy (cathect) nerve cells is not found anywhere in 'Gehirn'. On the one occasion that the 'Project' concept of the physical transfer of energy is mentioned in 'Gehirn', *the concept is attributed to Meynert*:

> [In Meynert's scheme] one of the principal pathways of the projection systems contains the fibres for voluntary movement and conscious sensation, the other contains the fibres for reflex (unconscious) *transference* of stimuli. [p. 56, this volume, our emphasis][8]

There is nothing in the article to suggest that Freud endorsed this concept. His own view was that:

> ... an excitation is *propagated [fortpflanzt]* from a specific point of the retina, by way of a specific nerve-fibre, up to a specific cellular element of the cortex. [p. 65, this volume, our emphasis]

Similarly, *Freud's conception of central inhibition in 'Gehirn' is very different to his 'side cathexis' conceptualization of inhibition in the 'Project'*. In the 'Project' Freud postulated no central inhibitory elements; he saw inhibition in terms of the lateral deviation of energy. In 'Gehirn' he identified cardio-inhibitory and vaso-constrictive centres in the medulla oblongata. At one point he made the following remark:

> As the essential components of these centres we . . . have to assume [the existence of] ganglion cells, the functional activities of which consist in the transmission of centrifugal impulses for cardio-inhibition and vaso-constriction. [p. 80, this volume]

This seems to imply that certain cells are exclusively inhibitory.

Thus 'Gehirn' supports Kanzer's and Mancia's 'psychological' interpretation of the 'Project'. In accordance with their view we do not see the conceptual continuity between the 'Project' and *The Interpretation of Dreams* as representing a neurophysiological influence upon psychoanalysis; we believe, instead, that the former is a remarkably early statement of the *psychological* theories first published in chapter 7 of the latter. We believe that this has significant implications for the current status of the metapsychology in general and the economic point of view in particular.

If the 'Project' model is really a psychology, however, then what is the meaning of its quasi-neurophysiological terminology and concepts? Perhaps the following statement (from chapter 7 of *The Interpretation of Dreams*) answers this question:[9]

> Since at our first approach to something unknown all that we need is the assistance of provisional ideas, I shall give preference in the first instance to hypotheses of the crudest and most concrete description. [1900a, p. 536]

## *4*

If Freud's earliest analytical theories were truly psychological, then which of the contemporary psychological 'schools' did he belong to? Was he influenced by Brentano, Herbart, or the associationists?

Andersson (1962) argued—and Amacher (1965, p. 65) tacitly agreed—that we do not find in Freud's articles from 1888 references to psychological processes other than those proposed by the associationists. If this is true, then the psychological significance of 'Gehirn' must be very limited. It was psychologically quite unoriginal and is only interesting insofar as it might demonstrate an associationist influence on Freud's thought (and this influence was recognized long ago by Dorer, 1932).

The basic principles of associationism are well known. The first principle is that *ideas* are the units of mental life (John Locke). Ideas are derived from sensations; they are, as it were, 'faint copies' of past sensations (David Hume). Accordingly, there are no innate ideas. The second principle is that there are both simple and complex ideas. Simple ideas associate to form complex ones in accordance with certain laws. The fundamental law of association states that any sensations $A$, $B$, or $C$, etc., by being associated with each other a sufficient number of times, come to link with their corresponding ideas $a$, $b$, and $c$, etc. in such a way that any future sensation $A$ alone, when it arouses its corresponding idea $a$, shall be able to bring to mind ideas $b$ and $c$ etc. as well. This is the law of contiguity. There was also the law of association by similarity and a few others. The associative links may be synchronous or successive and are therefore able to produce both compound ideas and trains of thought. The third principle is that the psychological processes of association are parallelled by almost identical physiological processes in the nerves and the brain (David Hartley). Thus vibrations in the nerves (i.e. sensations) give rise to miniature vibrations in the regions of the brain that correspond to the nerves (i.e. they give rise to ideas), and these link with each other by means of the association fibres.

Thus the most complex mental events are seen to be the products of simple associative neural mechanisms. It will be noted that these mechanisms are totally passive and environmentally determined.

Andersson's remark about the identity of Freud's early psychology with associationism was followed by the qualification that some Herbartian terms and viewpoints were applied as well, but he also believed that Freud was not aware of any difference between the Herbartian and the associationist conception and that the two were in many respects indistinguishable. This is an unusual claim, because dynamic Herbartian psychology is commonly contrasted with the passive psychology of the associationists (see Brett, 1912–21, pp. 549, 560; Boring, 1929, p. 253; Flügel, 1933, pp. 17, 23).

Johann Herbart did not analyse mental life into its elementary components, as did the associationists; he insisted that it can only be understood as a dynamic whole. He did not accept that ideas are passively associated but believed, instead, that they are actively drawn into or forced out of consciousness.

According to Herbart, ideas have both qualitative and quantitative characteristics. The quality (content) of each idea is invariable, but its quantitative aspect (its intensity or clarity) is in a constant state of flux and can vary between a state of complete inhibition and complete clarity. Between the two extremes there is a threshold of consciousness. Ideas exhibit a natural tendency towards the state of clarity and therefore constantly strive towards consciousness. This is expressed in that when (qualitatively) incompatible ideas interact, each makes an effort to conserve itself at the expense of the others. Thus the quantitative variation in the intensity of each idea arises out of the interaction between ideas. These relationships were expressed in a number of laws: Two simultaneous ideas of opposing content and equal intensity inhibit each other, and both remain below the threshold of consciousness. (Below the threshold ideas are not destroyed but merely yield from a state of reality to a state of tendency.) Two opposing ideas of unequal intensity hinder each other and contribute a resultant to consciousness. Where three incompatible ideas interact, one may be completely inhibited. Ideas that are compatible in terms of content cooperate in consciousness. If these ideas are from the same modality, they fuse. Considering the multiplicity of ideas, mutual opposition and inhibition are the rule in mental life. The composition of consciousness at any one moment is the result of the dynamic interplay between all ideas. Of those that remain below the threshold of consciousness, only the ideas that fit in with the unity of consciousness find so little resistance that they can rise above the threshold. This was Herbart's explanation for the limited range of consciousness or attention. Furthermore, Herbart claimed complete independence from physiology for psychology.

It seems clear that, although there are some continuities between Herbartianism and associationism, they represent fundamentally different approaches to the mind.

Silverstein (1985) disagreed with Andersson and Amacher and argued that Freud's early psychology had more in common with Brentano's 'act psychology' than with associationism.

Franz Brentano saw psychical phenomena as acts. What is psychical when one perceives, he argued, is not the object perceived but the act of seeing itself. Furthermore, psychical acts always have an object. The object is the intention of the act. Psychical acts, therefore, are not self-contained; they always refer to an external object. Physical events, on the other hand, are self-contained; they do not refer to anything. Thus Brentano declared a fundamental distinction between the psychical and the physical. This distinction is based on the presence or absence of intention. He also believed that all psychological theories of the unconscious are crypto-physiological (i.e. that they are based upon the concept of reflex action).

Brentano's 'act psychology' is usually contrasted with the 'content psychology' of the associationists and the early experimentalists. According to the 'content' school, the mind passively processes the material provided by the senses. According to the 'act' psychologists, it is an active, intentional agency. Adherents to the former view explained mental life in terms of mechanical (physicalist) causality; those who followed the latter approach believed, on the other hand, that the essence of the mental is neglected in any such reduction. This was the great dilemma facing psychology in the late nineteenth century when Freud wrote 'Gehirn'. Which view did he endorse?

In 'Gehirn' Freud conceived of the cortical physiological process in blatantly associationist terms (see p. 63, this volume).[10] The following conceptualization of the psychological process is also undeniably associationist:

> If a person reaches for a grape after he had seen it . . . the following psychical process *may* link with the . . . [physiological process:] The optical sensory perception of the [colour] blue, in a specific form, excites the ideas of the other attributes of the grape as well (and thereby those of [the grape] itself). Thirst-quenching capability also belongs to these attributes [which are] combined through previous repeated, simultaneous sensory perceptions and sensations. The ideas of thirst-quenching give rise to ideas of movements through which this [thirst-quenching]—as the imagined aim—can be reached. [p. 63, this volume]

This would seem to support the argument that Freud's earliest psychological views were totally derivative and similar to those of Meynert. However, the passage quoted above continues as follows:

> Thus, if all segments of the chain cross the threshold of consciousness, the psychical process is shaped in its *simplest* form. However, it may, on the one hand, become complicated by considerations of ethical and other nature, and, on the other hand, several or even all segments of the process can remain under the threshold of consciousness. [pp. 63, 64, this volume, our emphasis]

Thus, according to Freud, associationism can account for only the *simplest* of psychical phenomena. The Herbartian idea of a 'threshold of consciousness' explains some more complex events. Other Herbartian concepts contained in 'Gehirn' are: the equation of consciousness with attention (pp. 74, 75, this volume); the notion of a limited range of attention (p. 73, this volume); the distinction between the quantitative and qualitative components of mental life (p. 65, this volume),[11] the concept of a dynamic interplay between incompatible ideas producing a conscious resultant (p. 64, this volume); and the belief that psychological phenomena cannot be explained in purely physical terms (p. 62, this volume). These Herbartian concepts represent an approach to the mind that is fundamentally different to associationism (see above). Furthermore, the notion that *ethical* considerations might further complicate the mental process is entirely original and can only be described as 'Freudian'. An equally Freudian idea contained in 'Gehirn' is the postulate that the desire to reproduce an earlier experience of the satisfaction of a need is the prototypical psychical event, and the implication that thinking is 'experimental action' (pp. 63f, this volume). These ideas incorporate Brentano's axiom that psychical acts always refer to an object that embodies the intention of the act. The statement in 'Gehirn' (p. 64, this volume) that intentionality cannot be explained in physicalist, reductive terms can also be traced back to Brentano, but Freud's postulation of a psychical unconscious is incompatible with Brentano's scheme.

It seems that Andersson (1962), Amacher (1965), and Silverstein (1985) were all partly right. We can only conclude that Freud's earliest psychological theories were influenced by the views of Brentano *and* Herbart *and* the associationists, that they were identical with *none* of them, and that they also included some entirely original ideas. It appears that, from the very start, the future founder of psychoanalysis was an original thinker.

* * *

To conclude: 'Gehirn' is significant for psychoanalysis for four reasons:

1. It suggests that Freud conceptualized mental life independently of its organic substrate at the time when he was developing his earliest psychological theories.

2. It suggests that Freud did not endorse the now-discredited Meynertian models, which are so often alleged to have been incorporated into his psychoanalytical metapsychology; rather, that Freud was a Jacksonian neurologist at that stage and that his eariest psychological theories were therefore not based upon *any* neurological assumptions.
3. It supports the view that Freud's 'Project' was a truly psychological model. Therefore those aspects of *The Interpretation of Dreams* and the later psychoanalytical theory that can be traced back to the 'Project' cannot be criticized on neurological grounds and must be judged on their own psychological merits.
4. It suggests that Freud's earliest psychological theories were not directly derived from any of the prevailing psychological schools and were in many respects quite original.

## *NOTES*

1. Amacher did not use this actual term. However, he wrote that Freud's teachers described processes 'partly in physical and partly in psychological terms' (1965, p. 16) and that 'this unrestrained shifting from descriptions in terms of mind to descriptions in physical terms was characteristic of the work of Freud's teachers and of Freud. It is evident that they did not conceive of mental processes as in any detail independent of physical ones' (p. 17). This can only mean that they were identity theorists.
2. It also seems plausible to interpret Freud's (1888b2) statements to imply that he was a *non-reductive materialist* (see Davidson, 1980, for an account of this position), and numerous comments in Freud's later works would tend to support this interpretation. There is insufficient evidence in 'Gehirn' to decide whether Freud was a parallelist or a non-reductive materialist at that stage. Nevertheless, although these two philosophies disagree about the exact nature of the relationship between mind and body, *both* conceive of psychology as an independent science. Thus, from the practical point of view of the psychologist going about his research, there is little difference between them. Both approaches state that the

nature of the mind cannot be inferred from neurological knowledge—that this requires a proper *psychological* analysis. This would seem to be the essence of Freud's view.

3. We have focused on Meynert. In all important respects Meynert's views incorporated those of Freud's other Viennese neurological and physiological teachers.
4. Later he added a sixth, 'muscular' sense.
5. Here it is important to note that Freud (contra Holt, 1965) postulated spontaneously firing nerve cells in the 'Gehirn' article: 'they are capable of "automatic" excitation—[or] preferably "autochtonous" [excitation] [i.e. excitation] originating on the spot [where it is found]' (p. 81, this volume).
6. This does not imply that the model contained in *The Interpretation of Dreams* was a crypto-physiological one; on the contrary: the 'Project' was crypto-psychological (see below, in text).
7. It is true that Freud later returned (in an essentially metaphorical way) to the idea that external, quantitative stimuli impinge upon the psychical apparatus (see, e.g., Freud, 1920g). However, what we are trying to illustrate here is that Freud did not hold these views at the time that he was developing his fundamental psychoanalytical ideas—in *The Interpretation of Dreams*, for example—and that these views are therefore not 'crucial' to psychoanalysis at all. It is also important to note that when he returned to the metaphorical sensory-motor scheme, the pleasure principle itself simultaneously underwent radical revision and came to depend upon largely *qualitative* factors (see, e.g., ibid., pp. 8, 63; 1924c, p. 160).
8. This was the occasion of Freud's first published use of the word 'transference' [*Übertragung*]—a term that later came to have important technical psychoanalytical significance. According to Strachey, the word was first used in its psychoanalytical sense in 1895 (Breuer & Freud, 1895d, p. 302 n 1). Marx (1967, p. 819 n. 4) has since argued that Freud first used the word in *On Aphasia* (1891b, p. 56), but that this has been overlooked because Stengel mistranslated it as 'inference'. However, the word had an entirely non-analytical meaning in *On Aphasia*. We submit that 'Gehirn' not only contains the first appearance of the term in Freud's writings, but that its usage there is also not entirely unrelated to its later psychoanalytical sense.

   In 'Gehirn' Freud also used the terms 'projection' (cf. Stengel, 1953, p. xiii; Stengel, 1954, p. 86; Ornston, 1978, p. 119) and 'fixation' (cf. Strachey's discussion in Freud, 1892–93, p. 125n.) in their original, neuroscientific sense.
9. See also Solms & Saling, 1986, p. 405.

10. Here, incidentally, lie the roots of Freud's (1950a [1895]) 'law of association by simultaneity', which further demonstrates that the neuronic model in the 'Project' is primarily derived from psychological ideas.
11. If Freud endorsed Herbart's *psychological* theory that ideas have both qualitative and quantitative components, then this strengthens the argument that the economic point of view in psychoanalysis was not based upon hypothetical *physiological* considerations. (Freud was definitely familiar with Herbart's work from the very start of his career; see Jones, 1953.)

*SECTION ELEVEN*

# Significance of 'Aphasie' for psychoanalysis

There are two ways in which 'Aphasie' may be considered to be significant for psychoanalysis. The first has to do with the Meynert/Jackson controversy, the second with the psychoanalytical concept of 'parapraxis'.

*1*

We have already discussed the question whether the early Freud was Meynertian or Jacksonian. 'Aphasie' supports the answer suggested by our reading of 'Gehirn'.

It would seem reasonable to expect that a dictionary article on aphasia would present the currently orthodox definition and nosology of aphasia and a concise summary of the conventional view of the nature of the disorder. If it does not, then there is every reason to assume that the author of the article holds strongly unorthodox views (as was the case with 'Gehirn').

At the time that Freud wrote 'Aphasie' there were, roughly speaking, two schools of aphasiological thought. On the one hand, the localizationists assigned discreet areas of the left cerebral hemisphere to the various language functions on the basis of pathological anatomical findings. Their anti-localizationist opponents argued that language, as a complex higher mental function, is inseparable from other mental functions and consequently cannot be rigidly localized. Wernicke and Lichtheim—who explicitly based their theories on Meynert's scheme—championed the localizationist cause on the continent. Jackson opposed it from England.

### *The Meynertian view*

In 1861 Pierre Paul Broca reported a case with a small, circumscribed lesion and isolated loss of expressive speech. In view of the location of the lesion, he went on to proclaim the base of the third frontal gyrus of the left hemisphere as the 'speech centre'. Then, in 1874, in like fashion, Carl Wernicke assigned the ability to understand speech to the superior left temporal gyrus. Henceforth Broca's area was considered to be the centre for motor speech and Wernicke's area the centre for sensory speech. Wernicke explained the neural representation of language in terms of Meynert's 'cortico-centric' model. Thus, according to Wernicke, memory images of heard words accumulate in the cells of the superior left temporal gyrus because the fibres of the afferent speech tract terminate in those cells. Similarly, glosso-kinaesthetic word images—the products of articulatory movements—gradually occupy the cells in the posterior left frontal gyrus (Broca's area). This is because Broca's area is the origin of the efferent speech tract. The cells between Wernicke's and Broca's areas are functionless. This functionless gap is reserved for possible additional language acquisition (e.g. a second language). Next, association pathways develop between the auditory and the glosso-kinaesthetic word images. Thus the child learns to speak 'on' the association fibres between the sensory and motor speech areas.

In 1884 this theory was expanded by one of Wernicke's pupils, Ludwig Lichtheim. He postulated that there are seven different types of aphasia, each of which represents the destruction of a specific cell group or fibre tract. The doctrine was then formalized by Wernicke (1886), who designated the different aphasias as follows:

1. *Cortical motor aphasia,* caused by destruction of the motor speech centre (Broca's area);
2. *Cortical sensory aphasia,* resulting from damage to the sensory speech centre (Wernicke's area);
3. *Conduction aphasia* (paraphasia and inability to repeat heard words), which follows interruption of the association fibres connecting the above two centres;
4. *Transcortical motor aphasia* (impaired spontaneous speech, preserved repetition of heard words), which follows damage to non-speech cortical association fibres terminating in Broca's area;
5. *Transcortical sensory aphasia* (inability to understand speech, preserved repetition), resulting from damage to non-speech association fibres originating in Wernicke's area;
6. *Subcortical motor aphasia* (similar to [1]), caused by destruction of the efferent speech tract;
7. *Subcortical sensory aphasia* (similar to [2]), caused by damage to the afferent speech tract.

The classification also included *agraphia* (inability to write) and *alexia* (inability to read). These were thought to result from the destruction of hypothetical centres for visual word images and for cheiro-kinaesthetic word images. During the last decades of the nineteenth century, when Freud wrote 'Aphasie', the Wernicke–Lichtheim schema was the orthodox one in the German-speaking world. In fact, it was almost universally accepted.

### *The Jacksonian view*

Between 1864 and 1893, Jackson formulated a comprehensive alternative to localizationist aphasiology. His distinction between psychical and physical concepts was crucial to this alternative conception. Jackson differentiated the psychical phenomena of speech and language from the physical substrata serving those phenomena, and he considered the two aspects separately. From a psychological point of view, he argued, to speak is not merely to utter words but, rather, to *propositionize*. Propositional or *intellectual* speech can also be distinguished from *emotional* speech. He noted that although motor aphasics are speechless, they are not wordless, and they often retain isolated words and phrases. Their vocabularies usually include very automatic words like 'yes' and 'no', some other frequently used words and phrases, some swear-words, and a few other emotionally charged expressions. They tend to use these repetitively and indiscriminately, and for this reason Jackson called them 'recurrent utterances'. Recurrent utterances demonstrate that it is not the memory images of words but, rather, propositional speech that is lost in aphasia. He also noticed that aphasics often use certain words involuntarily but cannot reproduce them on demand and that they can involuntarily produce any tongue position but cannot articulate voluntarily. Here we recognize Jackson's analysis of pathology in terms of positive and negative symptomatology[1] and his conception of a hierarchy of nervous functions. With aphasia, propositional speech—one of the highest nervous functions—is lost (negative symptom), but lower nervous functions such as frequently used and therefore automatic words and phrases, involuntary expressions, and emotional speech are often retained (positive symptoms). Similarly, the second language of a bilingual aphasic will always suffer more than the first because it is acquired later and is less automatic. (This phenomenon is inexplicable in terms of the Wernicke–Lichtheim scheme.)

Jackson concluded that the localizationist doctrine of speech centres was unacceptable. He believed it to be the result of a confusion between concepts. First, Jackson argued, localizationism confuses the psychology of language with its physical basis. For example, it assumes that words (or units of language) are equivalent to cells (units of nervous tissue) without there being any justification for this assumption. Second, it confuses the localization of language functions with the location of damaged areas that impair those functions. When destruction of the superior left temporal gyrus leads to loss of the ability to understand speech, for example, this does not necessarily imply that that gyrus 'contains' that ability. It merely implies that the gyrus is an essential part of a potentially much larger nervous arrangement that subserves speech comprehension. According to Jackson, all parts of the cerebrum (including the right hemisphere) subserve language, although different parts serve different component language functions.

Jackson's views were little known and generally ignored at the time that Freud wrote 'Aphasie'.

Considering that the localizationist (Meynertian) scheme was the orthodox one in 1888, it is highly significant that Freud wrote in 'Aphasie' that although injuries to certain brain regions produce relatively pure forms of aphasia, it would be 'misleading' to conclude that these are centres for normal speech functions. His own view was completely incompatible with the Wernicke–Lichtheim doctrine:

> Remarkably, these 'centres' for speech are the most outlying districts of the speech field and border directly on the centres of other functions (the tongue and lips, the arm, hearing and sight in general), whereas lesions lying between the centres of the speech field still seem to produce complex speech disturbances. The so-called centres for speech are therefore probably merely the radiation areas of association bundles that reach the speech field from other regions. [p. 33, this volume]

The concept of speech centres was, of course, fundamental to Wernicke's and Lichtheim's doctrine. Equally fundamental was their notion of speech tracts, the interruption of which was believed to produce five distinct forms of aphasia (see above). Freud made no mention of these tracts. 'Aphasie' did not represent the Meynertian view.

In the very first paragraph of the article, aphasia was defined as 'a psychical illness' (p. 31, this volume). Accordingly, the speech function was dissected along psychological lines and Freud recommended that the physician should:

> analyse the more complicated aphasic disturbances through careful investigation in such a way that one can ascertain which connections between the individual elements of the word presentation, and between these and the idea of the designated object, are preserved or interrupted. [p. 35, this volume]

This was a flexible diagnostic alternative to the Wernicke–Lichtheim nosography (which Freud did not mention).[2] It is clear from this that Freud did not believe that the complex structure of speech pathology can be understood purely in terms of the location of the lesion. Rather, he believed that the nature of the disorder must be elucidated in each case by means of a careful *psychological* analysis of the symptoms. Elsewhere in the article he distinguished between 'natural or emotional speech (gestural speech) and artificial or articulate speech' and remarked that 'the latter succumbs to disturbances more frequently because it is acquired later' (p. 31, this volume). He also discussed the 'speech remnants' of the motor aphasic at some length (p. 34, this volume). All of these are Jacksonian ideas.

Clearly, Freud's 1888 aphasiology had more in common with Jackson's views than with the Wernicke–Lichtheim orthodoxy. The latter explicitly based their aphasiology upon Meynert's 'cortico-centric' teachings. Therefore, ***Freud's aphasiological views were implicitly anti-Meynertian.*** It seems that they were, in principle, Jacksonian. This need not necessarily mean, as Andersson (1962) has suggested, that he was under the *direct* influence of Jackson's writings at the time. Nevertheless, it definitely disconfirms Amacher's (1965) assertion that Freud made no significant departures from the neurology of his teachers, and all the negative implications that this has for psychoanalysis. If Freud rejected the Meynertian conception in 1888—years before he first used the psychoanalytical method—then it is difficult to see how this neurological conception could have had the baneful effect upon psychoanalysis that is so often attributed to it.

## 2

The second claim to significance for psychoanalysis of 'Aphasie' is perhaps a more direct one. *It contains Freud's very first mention of the 'parapraxis' concept*:

> The speech disturbance resulting from neurasthenic brain-fatigue is limited to the forgetting of individual concrete words and to the confusion of similar-sounding words in speech and is thus similar to the paraphasia that occurs in healthy people. [p. 36, this volume]

This is not only a clear reference to what he later called parapraxis, it also makes the direct link between this concept and neurosis, a link that he is traditionally thought to have first made ten years later.

According to Strachey (1960), we find the first mention of a parapraxis in a letter to Fliess of 26 August 1898. The letter contains the first actual psychoanalysis of a mistaken use of words and Freud's apparent discovery of the similarity between this sort of error and a neurotic symptom, although he added that this was something 'that I have long suspected' (Freud, 1954, p. 261). As Stengel (1953) has pointed out, however, he had already introduced the concept seven years earlier in *On Aphasia* (1891b, p. 13). On that occasion Freud noted the similarity between paraphasia and the speech errors that healthy people sometimes make. Stengel remarked that this reads like a prelude to the chapter on errors and slips of the tongue in *The Psychopathology of Everyday Life* (Freud, 1901b). The same can now be said about the above quotation from 'Aphasie', and we can add that the 1888 statement also reads like a prelude to Freud's (1898b) paper on forgetting and to the three chapters on forgetting in *The Psychopathology of Everyday Life*.

Strachey (1960) believed that Freud's special affection for parapraxes was due to the fact that they, along with dreams, were what enabled him to extend to normal mental life the discoveries that he had first made in connection with the neuroses. In a similar vein it can now be said that parapraxes enabled him to extend to normal mental life and psychopathology the discoveries that he had first made in connection with neurology.

* * *

To conclude: 'Aphasie' is significant for psychoanalysis, for two reasons:

1. It contradicts the view that Freud made no significant theoretical departures from the views of his neurological teachers. It also (albeit indirectly) contradicts the related argument that the erroneous neurological assumptions of Freud's teachers were incorporated into the psychoanalytical metapsychology.
2. It contains Freud's first mention of the concept of 'parapraxis'.[3]

## *NOTES*

1. Negative symptoms are the result of the lack of activity in damaged neural structures. Positive symptoms arise out of the activity of the intact lower-level structures that replace the functions of the damaged (higher) ones. In this way Jackson interpreted neurological symptomatology in dynamic terms.

2. The psychoanalyst will notice that this is also the origin of Freud's later (1915e) metapsychological distinction between 'word-presentations' and 'thing-presentations', which is traditionally traced back to the (1891b) monograph *On Aphasia* (Strachey, 1957a, 1957b).
3. 'Aphasie' also contains what seems to be *Freud's first published use of the term 'complex'*:

   > A 'word' is not a simple idea, but a complex that consists of four elements. [p. 32, this volume]

   Freud's usage of the term can clearly be traced back to the aphasiological theories of Charcot (see note 2, p. 36, this volume). This suggests that the Zurich school (Bleuler, Jung) were not single-handedly responsible for the introduction of this fundamental term into psychoanalysis (cf. Jones, 1955, pp. 34, 127; Strachey in Freud, 1941a [1892], p. 149 n. 2, and in Freud, 1950 [1895], p. 355 n. 5; Strachey, 1959, pp. 100–102).

*SECTION TWELVE*

# Significance of 'Aphasie' for neuroscience

Three years after Freud wrote 'Aphasie', he published his classic monograph *On Aphasia* (1891b) which earned him lasting fame in the neurological world (see part one). 'Aphasie' was his first and his only other published work on the subject of aphasia.

*1*

Most commentators agree on the nature of *On Aphasia*'s contribution to neuroscience. The following innovations are usually mentioned (cf. Brun, 1936; Jelliffe, 1937; Jones, 1953; Stengel, 1953; Spehlmann, 1953; Marx, 1966, 1967; etc.):

1. *On Aphasia* was one of the first studies to conceptualize aphasic symptomatology in terms of dynamic, functional factors rather than static, anatomical ones.

2. It criticized the orthodox Meynertian teaching that the body-periphery is directly 'projected' onto the cortex and argued instead that it is functionally 'represented' there.
3. It was one of the very few studies to recognize the value of Jackson's genetic approach to neurological pathology.
4. It contained the first comprehensive critique of the orthodox Wernicke–Lichtheim conception and classification of the aphasias.
5. It proposed that a single, continuous cortical area subserves all the different speech functions and that although the topography of this area is functionally diverse, it cannot be subdivided into a mosaic of discreet functional centres.
6. It was one of the first studies to claim that the localizationist and the dynamic neurological traditions are not irrevocably incompatible, that a belief in local functional variations in neural tissue does not necessarily imply the existence of discrete functional centres.
7. It was the first to realize that the prevailing 'language physiology' was merely a transposition of psychological insights into physiological terms.
8. It proposed one of the earliest purely psychological classifications of the aphasias.
9. It introduced the powerful 'agnosia' concept.
10. It foreshadowed the modern 'diaschisis' concept by interpreting certain traumatic symptoms in relation to distal cerebral shock effects.

Now, *it is our contention that 'Aphasie' directly anticipated most of the innovations traditionally attributed to the book On Aphasia.*

'Aphasie' contained a dynamic rather than a localizationist interpretation of aphasia. It described the localizationist doctrine of speech centres as 'misleading' (p. 32, this volume) and reinterpreted the significance of the so-called centres in terms of their dynamic relationships with other brain areas (cf [1] above).

Freud did not explicitly criticize the Meynertian conception of the organization of the brain in 'Aphasie' as he did in *On Aphasia*, but his approach in 'Aphasie' was incompatible with Meynert's teachings. Meynert's conception of the structure and functions of the cortex, when applied to aphasiology, could only make sense within a rigidly localizationist scheme. Wernicke and Lichtheim's scheme was explicitly based upon Meynert's model. Thus, by dismissing the localizationist approach as 'misleading' in 'Aphasie', Freud indirectly dismissed Meynert's model. This interpretation of 'Aphasie' is, of course, supported by the fact that Freud *was* directly critical of Meynert's model in 'Gehirn', which was written at the same time as 'Aphasie' (cf. [2] above).

'Aphasie' was implicitly Jacksonian. In it Freud called aphasia a 'psychical illness' (p. 31, this volume), he distinguished between emotional and artificial speech, and he interpreted aphasic symptomatology in genetic terms. He also attended to the 'positive symptoms' of the aphasic:

> In extreme cases the patient only has gestures, in others only individual syllables or words or even entire phrases, with which he answers everything. . . . The[se] speech remnants of the a[phasic] frequently have the character of interjection: 'Yes', 'No' . . . [etc.]. [p. 34, this volume]

All of these were Jacksonian ideas (cf. [3] above).

Although the Wernicke–Lichtheim scheme was not explicitly criticized in 'Aphasie', the doctrine of speech centres was dismissed as misleading, and the whole Wernicke–Lichtheim scheme was based upon this doctrine. Furthermore, the Wernicke–Lichtheim classification of the aphasias, which was almost universally accepted at the time, was conspicuously ignored in 'Aphasie' (cf. [4] above).

In 'Aphasie' Freud proposed that a single, continuous cortical area subserves all the different speech and language functions and that, although the topography of this area is functionally diverse, it cannot be subdivided into a mosaic of discrete functional centres. This unitary 'speech field' was defined as:

> . . . the island of Reil, with its surrounding convolution, which stretches from the frontal to the temporal ends of the hemisphere as the first frontal convolution, base of the central convolutions, inferior parietal lobule, and first temporal convolution. [p. 32, this volume]

In *On Aphasia* it was defined in exactly the same way (cf. [5] above).

Freud did not explicitly state in 'Aphasie' that the localizationist and dynamic approaches are ultimately reconcilable. However, he did argue that the so-called speech centres are probably merely the radiation areas of association bundles that reach the speech field from other regions (p. 33, this volume). These were the grounds for the claim in *On Aphasia* that a belief in local functional variation in neural tissue does not necessarily imply the existence of discrete functional centres. Although 'Aphasie' endorsed the dynamic approach, it nevertheless accepted that focal lesions in the four so-called centres do produce four different pure types of aphasia. It stated that the form of aphasia ultimately 'depends solely on the localization and extent of the established lesion in the speech field' (p. 35, this volume), but it simultaneously rejected the theoretical concept of speech centres and analysed the symptomatology psychologically. We can infer that Freud indirectly claimed in 'Aphasie' that the localizationist and dynamic approaches are ultimately reconcilable (cf. [6] above).

In 'Aphasie' a comprehensive, psychological classification of the aphasias was not proposed. However, it was stated that aphasic disturbances must be analysed in such a way that one can ascertain which links between the individual elements of the word-presentation, and between these and the object-presentation, are preserved or interrupted (p. 35, this volume). The psychological nosography in *On Aphasia* is based upon this exact scheme (cf. [8] above).

'Aphasie' anticipated *On Aphasia*'s adumbration of the 'diaschisis' concept:

> It is common to find motor a[phasia] in the first days after a left-sided apoplectic insult [and] for as long as the entire hemisphere continues to suffer under the consequences of the insult. Usually the speech disturbance soon diminishes. In such cases it can be perceived as an indirect focal symptom (p. 35, this volume; cf. [10] above).

We must agree with Schoenwald (1954), who believed that Freud's book *On Aphasia* merely 'fleshed out the bones of his article ['Aphasie'] with greater anatomical and physiological detail' (p. 123).

On this basis, we submit that *Freud's extraordinarily condensed dictionary article 'Aphasie' is a significant document in the history of aphasiology and neuropsychology.*

*2*

Here it should be noted that, although Freud's (1888b1) aphasiology was certainly unconventional, this need not *necessarily* imply that he was directly following Jackson's writings at the time (cf. Andersson, 1962). Although the ideas expressed in 'Aphasie' have much in common with Jackson's, his name is not mentioned, and there is no explicit reference to his aphasiology. The only reference is to Charcot. In view of the very abundant and generous references to Jackson in *On Aphasia*, this may be significant. In other words, Freud may have contributed his own sophisticated conceptualization of the neural organization of psychological functions. This could mean that he explicitly identified with Jackson in the later (1891) monograph *On Aphasia* because he realized that, in principle, his own views were compatible with Jackson's. If this is true, the importance of 'Aphasie' would increase. It is, indeed, an intriguing possibility that Freud's aphasiology was even more innovative than is currently recognized. We do not wish to overemphasize the thorny question of originality and influence. It is nevertheless important that we realize that Freud's dissidence with respect to the orthodox neurology of his time (and all that it represents today) can be established without this necessarily implying the wholesale subordination of his contributions to aphasiology to those of Jackson.

## *3*

It is an illuminating fact that Freud's (1888b1) aphasiology probably has more in common with modern neurodynamic formulations (Luria, 1970) than it had with the sanctioned localizationist 'mythology' of its time (Wernicke, 1886).[1]

Modern neurodynamic aphasiology takes the *psychology* of speech and language as its conceptual starting point, just as Freud did in 1888. Luria writes:

> Before one can properly investigate the nervous mechanisms underlying speech processes it is necessary to consider speech functions from the point of view of *psychology*. . . . Both the history of language and the psychology of speech . . . suggest that the processes underlying speech activity are considerably more complex than [nineteenth-century localizationist] diagrams would indicate. [1970, p. 80, our emphasis]

It is undeniable that we now know far more about the psychology of language than Freud did in 1888, but it was Freud's *injunction* that we should analyse individual aphasic symptoms in terms of their complex psychological structure, which so strikingly anticipated the modern neurodynamic approach. On this basis modern neurodynamic aphasiologists carefully distinguish between the localization of pathology and the localization of *function*, and the neural substrate of speech is conceptualized in terms of its dynamic functional organization within the diverse anatomical systems of the brain. This dynamic approach is succinctly described by Luria:

> It would . . . be improper . . . to conceive of the complex functional systems [involved in speech] as 'faculties' of limited cell groups and to 'localize' them in definite isolated areas of the brain. 'Localization of function' in this case becomes another problem, viz. the problem of the *dynamic distribution of functional systems in central regions of the nervous system* and especially in the cerebral cortex. Instead of conceptions of 'centres' for complex psychical processes there arise the concepts of *dynamic structures* or *constellations of cerebral zones*, each of which comprises part of the cortical portion of a given analyser and preserves its specific function, while participating in its own way in the organization of one or another form of activity. [1970, p. 20]

This is precisely what Freud argued in 'Aphasie' when he said that the so-called 'centres' are merely the 'radiations' of the primary parts of the auditory, visual, and motor analysers, and when he defined the 'speech field' as a continuous and yet heterogenous cortical zone (cf. Luria, 1970, pp. 29–33).

Considering that Luria has been described as 'the greatest neurological treasure of our time' (Sacks, 1985, p. 225), our decription of 'Aphasie' as a significant document in the history of aphasiology and neuropsychology seems to be justified.

* * *

To conclude: 'Aphasie' is significant for neuroscience for three reasons:

1. It anticipated most of the innovative ideas contained in *On Aphasia*, which is now an acknowledged classic.
2. It tentatively suggests that Freud may have arrived at his own anti-localizationist conception of aphasia independently of Jackson's direct influence.
3. It adumbrated the modern neurodynamic approach to higher cortical functions.

## *NOTE*

1. It could be argued that Freud's (1888b1, 1891b) aphasiology stood in the same relation to Wernicke's and Lichtheim's (Wernicke, 1886) as Luria's (1970) aphasiology now stands in relation to that of the so-called 'Boston School' (Benson & Geschwind, 1971; Goodglass & Kaplan, 1972). Our comparison between Freud's and modern aphasiologies, therefore applies only to the *neurodynamic* approach and not to that of the Boston School.

*SECTION THIRTEEN*

# Significance of 'Gehirn' for neuroscience

'Gehirn' was ostensibly a summary of the state of neuroanatomy and neurophysiology at the end of the nineteenth century, just before the discovery of the neurone. However, in certain important respects the article can be seen as having made original contributions to the neurological sciences.

*1*

It has been suggested that 'Gehirn' was a preparatory study for Freud's 1891b book on aphasia (Spehlmann, 1953; Vogel, 1953). Herein lies its first claim to neuroscientific significance. This is because 'Gehirn' laid the *anatomical* foundations for that classic contribution to neurology. The basic principle upon which all the arguments in *On Aphasia* were based was that the body-periphery is functionally represented in the cortex rather than being somatotopically projected there. The anti-Meynertian scheme in 'Gehirn'—

which assigned important integratory functions to the subcortical grey masses—provided the anatomical justification for that basic principle (cf. Freud, 1891b, pp. 44–66).

## 2

The anatomical model proposed in 'Gehirn' is also significant in its own right. This is because it was *a comprehensive alternative to the orthodox, but discredited Meynertian scheme*. Freud wrote in 'Gehirn' that the Meynertian conception of the structure of the brain had been 'shattered', but that his scheme could still not be replaced by another general conception (pp. 58, this volume). Nevertheless Freud immediately proceeded to propose just such an alternative model:

> The central nervous system is to be considered as a union of grey masses, which are directly or indirectly linked with *each other* [as opposed to the periphery] by fibre bundles. Amongst these [grey masses], the grey of the spinal cord with its continuation in the oblongata . . . is the *only* grey mass that has a direct relationship with the periphery. . . . There are, therefore, no fibre systems that by-pass the spinal cord and ascend directly to higher-lying grey substances. . . . It is further evident that the larger part of the medullated fibres of the spinal cord are used to link its own grey substances, and [that] only a small part are given to the subsequent conduction of impulses to other grey substances. . . . [Similarly,] the larger number of fibre bundles in the cerebrum are its own association fibres; only a small part serve association with other grey masses. If one retains the [Meynertian] name 'projection system' for the links of the cerebrum with the spinal cord, then the number of fibres [in that system] is eclipsed by the amount in the remaining [non-projection] systems. The majority of fibre systems in the brain stem [also] serve to link grey masses with each other. [p. 58, this volume, our emphasis]

Freud went on to propose a new classification of the fibre systems to replace Meynert's projection/association scheme. The modern neuroanatomist would find little in the above model with which he could disagree. It is interesting to compare the quotation with the following passage by Meynert:

> The relation of the fore-brain to the other parts of the cerebral mechanism is easily understood. To this end we may recall the structure of the retina, which constitutes a hollow into which the visual rays from the external world are, as it were, entrapped. And, in the same way, we may look upon each half of the cortex of the fore-brain as a concave organ, duplicated in parts, enveloping *all* the nerve tracts, which conduct to it the impressions from the outer world. . . . Just as the mollusca possesses tentacles which protrude toward the outer world, and claws by means of which they take possession of their booty, so this complicated protoplasmic organism, the prosencephalic cortex, possesses centripetally conducting processes,—the sensory fibres of the nervous system—which we may consider its tentacles, and motor fibres, which are its claws. [1885, p. 139, our emphasis]

The modern neuroscientist would find little in this 'mythology' with which he could agree. Although it would be incorrect to argue that our present views are actually derived from Freud's, it is nevertheless a significant fact that the conception of the structure of the brain that he proposed to replace the Meynertian doctrine is still viable today, a full one hundred years later.

## *3*

The methodology upon which Freud's model was based was also a significant advance. Meynert described his scientific method as follows:

> A mechanism may operate before us without our recognizing the exact relation between its function and its architecture. But, on the other hand, if we are acquainted with the principles upon which the mechanism operates, *we may infer its function from its structure,* regarding the former as the natural outcome of the latter. This method of reasoning would be applicable to the brain, even though the principles involved in its activity were entirely unknown. [1885, p. 138, our emphasis]

On this very dubious basis Meynert proceeded to develop his complete theory of brain function upon essentially *anatomical* evidence. Thus his passive reflex physiological model was derived from his cortico-centric anatomical scheme. We have already seen that, in terms of this physiological model, the whole psychological sphere is merely one link in a chain of reflex physical events (i.e. the cortical link). Therefore, for Meynert, psychology is ultimately reducable to anatomy. This fact is made abundantly clear in Meynert's preface to his psychiatric textbook:

> The reader will find no other definition of 'Psychiatry' in this book but the one given on the title page [*Psychiatry: A Clinical Treatise on Diseases of the Forebrain based upon a study of its Structure, Functions, and Nutrition*] . . . were I to give a functional designation to the morbid affectations of the fore-brain, I would choose the term 'Diseases of the Mind'. [1885, p. v]

Freud asserted in 'Gehirn' that psychology could not be reduced to anatomy (or physiology). Thus ideas could not be localized in nerve cells, discrete areas of neural tissue could not be assigned complex psychological functions, and nerve tracts could not be differentiated in terms of the psychological processes they were presumed to subserve. All these considerations were fundamental to the radical new interpretation of the aphasias that he proposed in 1891. Marx (1967) has argued that Freud's distinction between psychological and anatomical concepts (which he thought Freud first made in *On Aphasia*) exposed *the* 'major fallacy' of nineteenth-century neuroscience. Meynert's 'brain mythology' was succeeded by more modest, more cautiously empirical, and more philosophically sophisticated investigations into the neural organization of psychological functions. This development has culminated in modern dynamic neuropsychology, in which purely psychological analysis has pride of place as the principal investigative method. 'Gehirn' (like Freud's work on aphasia) *can rightfully be included amongst those late nineteenth-century texts that signalled the beginning of this new neuroscientific era.*

* * *

To conclude: 'Gehirn' is significant for neuroscience, for three reasons:

1. It laid the anatomical foundations for the theoretical arguments contained in *On Aphasia*—Freud's classic contribution to the field.
2. It proposed a comprehensive alternative to the then-orthodox Meynertian scheme.
3. It escaped the major methodological flaw of nineteenth-century neuroscience.

*SECTION FOURTEEN*

# Summary and conclusions

**We have been able to reach the following general conclusions in this book:**

**'Aphasie' and 'Gehirn' were written by Sigmund Freud. He conceived them during a crucial phase in the development of his thought, whilst he was making his first systematic psychological observations and constructing his first psychological theories. The articles suggest that, during this crucial phase, his approach was implicitly Jacksonian and explicitly anti-Meynertian. This has important implications for psychoanalysis.**

**Freud did not endorse Meynert's (anatomical) 'corticocentric' and (physiological) 'hydraulic reflex' models of neural and mental functioning. Freud's later psychoanalytical metapsychology (especially its economic aspect) has often been criticized in terms of its supposed derivation from these models. This now seems inappropriate. In addition, it is evident that Freud, like Jackson, conceptualized psychological processes independently of their organic substrate. This means that, from the very start, his psychological theoriza-**

tion was probably not derived from *any* neurophysiological system. In this respect the 1888 articles also throw new light on the 'Project for a scientific psychology' and chapter 7 of *The Interpretation of Dreams*. They contain material that strongly supports the purely 'psychological' interpretation of those early metapsychological formulations.

The articles also suggest that although Freud's germinal conceptualizations were influenced from many directions, there is much in them that was original. He appears not to have belonged to any of the prevailing psychological schools. Some standard psychoanalytical concepts can also be traced back to this period. The notion of parapraxis was first introduced in 'Aphasie', and dynamic, unconscious psychical processes were first postulated in 'Gehirn'.

The articles are also interesting from a neuroscientific point of view. They contained a comprehensive theoretical alternative to the then-orthodox Meynertian conception of brain structure and function. A new anatomical model was proposed in 'Gehirn'. This provided the framework within which *On Aphasia*—Freud's classical contribution to neurology—was written. Most of the radically important aphasiological views expressed in that work were clearly adumbrated in 'Aphasie'. In many respects Freud's 1888 views have more in common with modern neurodynamic concepts (Luria) than with the now discredited systems of his nineteenth-century contemporaries.

## REFERENCES


Amacher, P. (1965). Freud's neurological education and its influence on psychoanalytic theory. *Psychological Issues, 4* (4) (Monograph 16).

______. (1974). The concepts of the pleasure principle and infantile erogenous zones shaped by Freud's neurological education. *The Psychoanalytic Quarterly, 43*: 218–223.

Andersson, O. (1962). *Studies in the Prehistory of Psychoanalysis: The Etiology of Psychoneuroses and Some Related Themes in Sigmund Freud's Scientific Writings and Letters, 1886–1896.* Stockholm: Svenska Bokforlaget.

Aronsohn, E., & Sachs, J. (1884). Ein Wärmecentrum im Grosshirn. *Deutsche medische Wochenschrift, 10*: 823–825.

______. (1885–86). Die Beziehungen des Gehirns zur Körperwärme und zum Fieber. *Archiv für die gesamte Physiologie, 37*: 232–301.

Benson, F., & Geschwind, N. (1971). The aphasias and related disturbances. In A. Baker & L. Baker (eds.), *Clinical Neurology.* Hagerstown: Harper & Row.

Bernfeld, S. (1944). Freud's scientific beginnings. *The American Imago, 6*: 162–196.

______. (1951). Sigmund Freud, M.D. 1882–1885. *The International Journal of Psycho-Analysis, 32*: 204–217.

Bernfeld, S., & Cassirer-Bernfeld, S. (1952). Freud's first year in practice, 1886–1887. *Bulletin of the Menninger Clinic, 16*: 37–49.

Bettelheim, B. (1983). *Freud and Man's Soul*. London: Chatto and Windus.

Boring, E. (1929). *A History of Experimental Psychology*. New York: Century.

Brandt, L. (1961). Some notes on English Freudian terminology. *Journal of the American Psychoanalytic Association, 9*: 331–339.

Brazier, M. (1959). The historical development of neurophysiology. In J. Field, H. Magoun, & V. Hall (eds.), *Handbook of Physiology*, Section 1; *Neurophysiology*, Volume 1, pp. 1–58. Washington, DC: American Physiological Society.

Brett, G. (1912–21). *History of Psychology* (3 volumes). London: Allen and Unwin.

Broca, P. (1861). Perte de la parole. Ramollissement chronique et destruction partielle du lobe antérieur gauche du cerveau. *Bulletin de la Societe d'Anthropologique, 2*: 235–238.

Brull, H. (1975). A reconsideration of some translations of Sigmund Freud. *Psychotherapy: Theory, Research and Practice, 12*: 273–279.

Brun, R. (1936). Sigmund Freuds Leistungen auf dem Gebiete der organischen Neurologie. *Archiv für Neurologie und Psychiatrie, 37*: 201–207.

Byck, R. (1974). Sigmund Freud and cocaine. Introduction to Freud's *Cocaine Papers*, pp. xvii–xxxix. Miami, FL: University of Miami Press.

Charcot, J.-M. (1886). *Neue Vorlesungen über die Krankheiten des Nervensystems insbesondere über Hysterie* (trans. S. Freud). Leipzig and Vienna: Toeplitz & Deuticke.

Davidson, D. (1980). *Essays on Actions and Events*. New York and London: Oxford University Press.

Dorer, M. (1932). *Historische Grundlagen der Psychoanalyse*. Leipzig: Felix Meiner Verlag.

Eissler, K. (1971). *Talent and Genius: The Fictitious Case of Tausk contra Freud*. New York: Quadrangle Books.

Exner, S. & Paneth, J. (1887). Über Sehstörungen nach Operationen am Vorderhirn. *Archiv für die gesamten Physiologie, 40*: 62–64.

Flügel, J. (1933). *A Hundred Years of Psychology, 1833–1933*. London: Duckworth.

Forrester, J. (1980). *Language and the Origins of Psychoanalysis*. London: Macmillan.

Freud, S. (1882a). Über den Bau der Nervenfasern und Nervenzellen beim Flusskrebs. *Sitzungsberichte der kaiserlichen Akademie der Wissenschaften (Wien)*, Mathematisch-Naturwissenschaftliche Klasse, *78*: 81–167.

———. (1884b). Eine neue Methode zum Studium des Faserverlaufs im Zentralnervensystem. *Zentralblatt für die medizinischen Wissenschaften, 22*: 161–163.

———. (1884c). A new histological method for the study of nerve-tracts in the brain and spinal chord. *Brain, 7*: 86–88.

———. (1884d). Eine neue Methode zum Studium des Faserverlaufs im Zentralnervensystem. *Archiv für Anatomie und Physiologie (Anatomische Abtheilung), 3*: 453–460.

———. (1884f [1882]). Die Struktur der Elemente des Nervensystems. *Jahrbücher für Psychiatrie und Neurologie, 5*: 221–229.

———. (1884–87). *Cocaine Papers*, edited by R. Byck. New York: Stonehill Publishing Co. (1974).

———. (1885d). Zur Kenntnis der Olivenzwischenschicht. *Neurologischer Zentralblatt, 4*: 268–270.

———. (1886c). Über den Ursprung des Nervus acusticus. *Monatsschrift für Ohrenheilkunde* (Neue Folge), *20*: 245–251, 277–282.

———. (1886d). Observation of a severe case of hemi-anaesthesia in a hysterical male. *SE, 1*: 24–31.

———. (1886e). Preface to the translation of Charcot's *Lectures on the Diseases of the Nervous System*. *SE, 2*: 19–22.

———. (1887a). Review of Averbeck's 'Die akute Neurasthenie.' *SE, 1*: 35.

———. (1887b). Review of Weir Mitchell's *Die Behandlung gewisser Formen von Neurasthenie und Hysterie*. *SE, 1*: 36.

———. (1887f). Das Nervensystem. In E. Buchheim (ed.), *Ärzliche Versicherungsdiagnostik* (Abschnitt 5). Vienna: Alfred Holder.

———. (1888b1). Aphasie. In A. Villaret (ed.), *Handwörterbuch der gesamten Medizin, Volume 1* (pp. 88–90). Stuttgart: Ferdinand Enke Verlag.

_______. (1888b2). Gehirn. In A. Villaret (ed.), *Handwörterbuch der gesamten Medizin, Volume 1* (pp. 684–697). Stuttgart: Ferdinand Enke Verlag.

_______. (1888b3). Hysteria. *SE, 1*: 37–57.

_______. (1888b4). Hystero-epilepsy. *SE, 1*: 58–59.

_______. (1888–89). Preface to the translation of Bernheim's *Suggestion. SE, 1*: 73–85.

_______. (1891b). *On Aphasia. A Critical Study*. New York: International Universities Press (1953).

_______. (1892–93). A case of successful treatment by hypnotism. *SE, 1*: 117–128.

_______. with Breuer, J. (1893a). On the psychical mechanism of hysterical phenomena: Preliminary communication. *SE* 2.

_______. (1893c). Some points for a comparative study of organic and hysterical motor paralyses. *SE, 1*: 157–172.

_______. (1893f). Charcot. *SE, 3*: 9–24.

_______. (1894a). The neuro-psychoses of defence. *SE, 3*: 43–61.

_______. (1895b [1894]. On the grounds for detaching a particular syndrome from neurasthenia under the description 'anxiety neurosis'. *SE, 3*: 85–118.

_______ with Breuer (1895d). *Studies on Hysteria. SE, 2*.

_______. (1897a). *Infantile Cerebral Paralysis*. Miami, FL: University of Miami Press (1968).

_______. (1897b). Abstracts of the scientific writings of Dr. Sigm. Freud, 1877–1897. *SE, 1*: 225–257.

_______. (1898b). The psychical mechanism of forgetfulness. *SE, 3*: 288–297.

_______. (1900a). *The Interpretation of Dreams. SE, 4* and *5*.

_______. (1900b). Cerebrale Kinderlähmung. *Jahresbericht über die Leistungen und Fortschriftte auf dem Gebiete der Neurologie und Psychiatrie, 3*: 611–618.

_______. (1901b). *The Psychopathology of Everyday Life. SE, 6*.

_______. (1905e[1901]). Fragment of an analysis of a case of hysteria. *SE, 7*: 3–112.

_______. (1911c[1910]). Psycho-analytic notes on an autobiographical account of a case of paranoia (Dementia paranoides). *SE, 12*: 9–82.

_______. (1915e). The unconscious. *SE, 14*: 161–204.

_______. (1916–17). *Introductory Lectures on Psycho-Analysis. SE, 15*: 15–239.

______. (1920g). *Beyond the Pleasure Principle. SE, 18*: 3–64.

______. (1924c). The economic problem of masochism. *SE, 19*: 157–170.

______. (1925d). *An Autobiographical Study. SE, 20*: 3–70.

______. (1940a). *An Outline of Psycho-Analysis. SE, 23*: 141–207.

______. (1950a). *Aus den Anfängen der Psychoanalyse: Briefe an Wilhelm Fliess, Abhandlungen und Notizen aus den Jahren 1887–1902,* edited by M. Bonaparte, A. Freud & E. Kris. London: Imago Publishing Co. (trans.: Freud, 1954).

______. (1941a [1892]). Letter to Josef Breuer. *SE, 1*.

______. (1950a [1895]). Project for a scientific psychology. *SE, 1*: 281–391.

______. (1954). *The Origins of Psycho-Analysis, Letters to Wilhelm Fliess, Drafts and Notes: 1887–1902,* edited by M. Bonaparte, A. Freud & E. Kris. London: Imago Publishing Co.

______. (1960a). *Letters of Sigmund Freud, 1873–1939,* edited by E. Freud. London: The Hogarth Press.

______. (1985). *The Complete Letters of Sigmund Freud to Wilhelm Fliess,* 1887–1904, edited by J. Masson. Cambridge and London: Harvard University Press.

______ & Darkschewitsch, L. (1886). Über die Beziehung des Strickkörpers zum Hinterstrang und Hinterstrangkern nebst Bemerkungen über zwei Felder der Oblongata. *Neurologischer Zentralblatt, 5*: 121–129.

______ & Rie, O. (1891a). Klinische Studie über die halbseitige Cerebrallähmung der Kinder. *Beiträge zur Kinderheilkunde, Volume 3,* edited by M. Kassowitz. Vienna: Moritz Perles Verlag.

Fullinwider, S. (1893). Sigmund Freud, John Hughlings Jackson, and speech. *Journal of the History of Ideas, 44*: 151–158.

Gill, M., & Holzman, P. (eds.) (1976). *Psychology versus Metapsychology*. New York: International Universities Press.

Goldstein, K. (1912). Die zentrale Aphasie. *Neurologischer Zentralblatt, 31*: 739–751.

Goodglass, H., & Kaplan, E. (1972). *The Assessment of Aphasia and Related Disorders*. Philadelphia, PA: Lea and Febiger.

Grinstein, A. (1956). *The Index of Psychoanalytic Writings, Volume 1*. New York: International Universities Press.

Grossman, W. (1986). Before the pleasure principle: Translation and its vicissitudes (letter to the editor). *Journal of the American Psychoanalytic Association, 134*: 1211–1221.

Heilman, K. and Valenstein, E. (1979). *Clinical Neuropsychology*. New York and Oxford: Oxford University Press.

Holt, R. (1965). A review of some of Freud's biological assumptions and their influence on his theories. In N. Greenfield & W. Lewis (eds.), *Psychoanalysis and Current Biological Thought*, pp. 93–124. Madison and Milwaukee, WI: University of Wisconsin Press.

Jackson, J. (1884). Evolution and dissolution of the nervous system. In J. Taylor (ed.), *Selected Writings of John Hughlings Jackson, Volume 2* (pp. 45–75). London: Hodder and Stoughton.

Jelliffe, S. (1937). Sigmund Freud as a neurologist. Some notes on his earlier neurobiological and clinical neurological studies. *Journal of Nervous and Mental Disease, 85*: 696–711.

Jones, E. (1953). *Sigmund Freud: Life and Work, Volume 1*. London: The Hogarth Press.

______. (1955). *Sigmund Freud: Life and Work, Volume 2*. London: The Hogarth Press.

Kanzer, M. (1973). Two prevalent misconceptions about Freud's 'Project'. *The Annual of Psychoanalysis, 1*: 88–103.

Kolb, B., & Whishaw, I. (1980). *Fundamentals of Human Neuropsychology*. San Francisco, CA: W. H. Freeman and Co.

Kris, E. (1950a). Introduction to Freud's *Aus den Anfängen der Psychoanalyse* (M. Bonaparte, A. Freud & E. Kris, eds.), (pp. 5–56). London: Imago Publishing Co. (trans.: Kris, 1954).

______ (1950b). The significance of Freud's earliest discoveries. *The International Journal of Psycho-Analysis, 31*: 108–116.

______ (1954). Introduction to Freud's *The Origins of Psychoanalysis* (M. Bonaparte, A. Freud & E. Kris, eds.), (pp. 3–47). London: Imago Publishing Co.

Ludwig, C. (1861). Über die Kräfte die Nervenprimitivenrohr. *Wien medische Wochenschrift, 46*: 47.

Luria, A. (1970). *Traumatic Aphasia. Its Syndromes, Psychology and Treatment*. The Hague and Paris: Mouton.

______. (1980). *Higher Cortical Functions in Man* (2nd edition, revised and expanded). New York: Basic Books.

Mahler, M. & McDevitt, J. (1982). Thoughts on the emergence of the sense of self, with particular emphasis on the body self. *Journal of the American Psychoanalytic Association, 30*: 827–848.

Mancia, M. (1983). Archaeology of Freudian thought and the history of neurophysiology. *The International Review of Psycho-Analysis, 10*: 185–192.

Martin, H. & Brooker, W. (1878). The influence of stimulation of the midbrain upon the respiratory rhythm of the mammal. *Journal of Physiology, 1*: 370–376.

Marx, O. (1966). Aphasia studies and language theory in the 19th century. *Bulletin of the History of Medicine, 40*: 328–349.

_______. (1967). Freud on aphasia: An historical analysis. *American Journal of Psychiatry, 124*: 815–825.

McCarley, R. & Hobson, J. (1977). The neurobiological origins of psychoanalytic dream theory. *The American Journal of Psychiatry, 134*: 1211–21.

Meynert, T. (1885). *Psychiatry: A Clinical Treatise on Diseases of the Fore-Brain based upon A Study of its Structure, Functions, and Nutrition*. New York and London: G. P. Putnam's Sons.

Ornston, D. (1978). On projection. A study of Freud's usage. *Journal of the American Psychoanalytic Association, 26*: 117–166.

_______. (1985). Freud's conception is different from Strachey's. *Journal of the American Psychoanalytic Association, 33*: 379–412.

Pribram, K. (1962). The neuropsychology of Sigmund Freud. In A. Bachrach (ed.), *Experimental Foundations of Clinical Psychology* (pp. 442–468). New York: Basic Books.

Riese, W. (1958). Freudian concepts of brain function and brain disease. *The Journal of Nervous and Mental Disease, 127*: 287–307.

Sacks, O. (1985). *The Man Who Mistook His Wife for a Hat*. London: Duckworth.

Schafer, R. (1976). *A New Language for Psychoanalysis*. New Haven and London: Yale University Press.

Schoenwald, R. (1954). A turning point in Freud's life: 'Zur Auffassung der Aphasien'. *Osiris, 7*: 119–126.

Silverstein, B. (1985). Freud's psychology and its organic foundation: Sexuality and mind–body interactionism. *Psychoanalytic Review, 72*: 203–228.

Solms, M. & Saling, M. (1986). On psychoanalysis and neuroscience: Freud's attitude to the localizationist tradition. *The International Journal of Psycho-Analysis, 67*: 397–416.

Spehlmann, R. (1953). *Sigmund Freuds neurologische Schriften*. Berlin, Göttingen, Heidelberg: Springer Verlag.

Stengel, E. (1953). Introduction to Freud's *On Aphasia* (pp. ix–xv). New York: International Universities Press.

———. (1953). A re-evaluation of Freud's *On Aphasia*. Its significance for psychoanalysis. *The International Journal of Psycho-Analysis, 35*: 85–89.

———. (1964). Hughlings Jackson's influence in psychiatry. *British Journal of Psychiatry, 109*: 348–355.

Storch, E. (1903). Der aphasische Symptomencomplex. *Monatsschrift für Psychiatrie und Neurologie, 13*: 597–622.

Strachey, J. (1957a). Editor's note to Freud's 'The unconscious'. *SE, 14*: 161–165.

———. (1957b). Appendix C to Freud's 'The unconscious': 'Words and things.' *SE, 14*: 209–215.

———. (1959). Editor's note to Freud's 'Psycho-analysis and the establishment of the facts in legal proceedings.' *SE, 9*: 99–102.

———. (1960). Editor's introduction to Freud's 'The psychopathology of everyday life'. *SE, 6*: ix–xiv.

———. (1962). Editor's note to Freud's 'Abstracts of the scientific writings of Dr. Sigm. Freud.' *SE, 3*: 225–226.

———. (1966a). Editor's note to Freud's Preface to the translation of Charcot's *Lectures on the Diseases of the Nervous System*. *SE, 1*: 19–20.

———. (1966b). Editor's note to Freud's 'Hysteria'. *SE, 1*: 39–40.

———. (1966c). Editor's note to Freud's papers on hypnotism and suggestion. *SE, 1*: 63–69.

———. (1966d). Appendix C to Freud's 'Project for a scientific psychology': 'The nature of Q'. *SE, 1*: 392–397.

———. (1974). Freud bibliography. *SE, 24*: 47–82.

Sulloway, F. (1979). *Freud, Biologist of the Mind: Beyond the Psychoanalytic Legend*. London: Andre Deutsch and Burnett Books.

Thiele, R. (1928). Aphasie, Apraxie, Agnosie. In O. Bumke (ed.), *Handbuch der Geisteskrankheiten, Volume 2* (pp. 245–339). Berlin: Springer Verlag.

Triarhou, L., & Del Cerro, M. (1985). Freud's contribution to neuroanatomy. *Archives of Neurology, 42*: 282–287.

Tyson, A., & Strachey, J. (1956). A chronological handlist of Freud's works. *The International Journal of Psycho-Analysis, 37*: 19–33.

Upson, H. (1888). On gold chloride as a staining agent for nerve tissues. *Journal of Nervous and Mental Disease, 15*: 685–689.

Villaret, A. (ed.) (1888/1891). *Handwörterbuch der gesamten Medizin* (2 volumes). Stuttgart: Ferdinand Enke Verlag.

Vogel, G. (1978). An alternative view of the neurobiology of dreaming. *The American Journal of Psychiatry, 135*: 1531–1538.

Vogel, P. (1953). Eine erste, unbekannt gebliebene Darstellung der Hysterie von Sigmund Freud. *Psyche, 7*: 486–500.

Walsh, K. (1978). *Neuropsychology: A Clinical Approach*. Edinburgh, London, New York: Churchill Livingstone.

Wasserman, M. (1984). Psychoanalytic dream theory and recent neurobiological findings about REM sleep. *Journal of the American Psychoanalytic Association, 32*: 831–846.

Wernicke, C. (1886). Einige neuere Arbeiten über Aphasie. *Fortschritte der Medizin, 4*: 377–463.

# INDEX